Fear
Anxiety
AND
Wellness

JOURNEY TO A
HEART AT PEACE

Too often, subjects of vital importance are addressed with a segmented approach or from just a few perspectives. *Fear, Anxiety and Wellness* is a stunning exception to this norm that melds science, reason, psychology, and faith. Fear is at the root of all that diminishes human potential and a life of purpose, passion, and service. Dr. Eckrich's book gets at the foundational underpinnings of fear from a multidisciplinary approach, which includes a Christian understanding of fear. While addressing the causes of fear, he also offers effective strategies to deal with fear and encourage our journey to wellness through Christ. *Fear, Anxiety and Wellness* is a powerful invitation to confront fear and to live each day with a faith that reminds us, "Perfect love casts out all fear." As a former psychologist and current pastor, it is evident that pondering and acting upon Dr. Eckrich's words will move the reader further down the path that God intends for each of us.

The Rev. Dr. Robert DeWetter
Episcopal Priest and Clinical Psychologist
Senior Pastor, Snowmass Chapel

As a regional and national church leader for almost 20 years, *Fear, Anxiety and Wellness* strikes a chord in my mind and heart. Dr. Eckrich has created a resource that will be most helpful to individuals, congregations, and organizations torn apart by internal strife, including regional ecclesiastical judicatories and national church bodies. Chapter Ten: "Facing Fear of Congregational and Denominational Conflict" is a must read for such troubled entities. Serious organizational strife can be healed only through the power of the Word of God, embellished by medical and psychological insight under the Spirit's guidance. My experience in ecclesiastical supervision prompts my appreciation and commendation for Dr. Eckrich's contribution to conquering the fear and anxiety that exacerbates congregational and denominational conflict. This book addresses this daunting task from both a practical and theological viewpoint. Get this book, read it, and thank God for it!

Rev. Dr. Gerald Kieschnick
President Emeritus, Lutheran Church—Missouri Synod
Inheritance Legacy Consultant, Lutheran Foundation of Texas

Eckrich's book is rich with helpful anecdotes and commentary from his personal life and clinical practice as he explores the causes and cures for this diagnosis. It is a privilege to have access to the insights of a Christian physician with sensitivities to the biological *and* spiritual underpinnings of both illness and the process of healing. The book will be of particular value for those who have suffered with anxiety as well as those who love or have befriended an anxious soul.

Beverly K. Yahnke, Ph.D.
Executive Director for Christian Counsel
DOXOLOGY

Dr. Eckrich really gets it! Pastors have worked through their fear of public speaking (often to our dismay) but are plagued by the myriad other anxiety-causing forces of a life in ministry— whether "real or imagined," as John would say. The in-depth but easily readable insights into the medical and physiological nature of our anxieties, combined with John's Christ-centered prescription for remediation are a treasure trove for anyone, especially pastors fighting their way through this nightmare. I know this very well from my own 30 years of handling my fears often quite poorly. But with John's guidance I'm rediscovering the joy of an (almost) anxiety-free ministry. Thanks, John! This resource will benefit the thousands of pastors you've already blessed and a generation to follow!

Rev. Dr. Darrell W. Zimmerman
Vice President and Program Director, Grace Place Wellness Ministries

Dr. Eckrich explores the depths of fear and anxiety as a physical, emotional, and spiritual human condition. He brings to his writing a lifetime of experience as a physician who is also a patient and devout Christian, retreat leader, and lifelong learner. The author reaches out to readers seeking an understanding of how fear affects a person and provides a faith-based prescription for living creatively with fear and anxiety. I would recommend this book as an educational resource to Christians struggling with fear and anxiety and to those who love and care for them. It is also an excellent resource for faith community nurses, pastoral caregivers, and congregational health volunteers.

Mary R. Jacob, Ed.D., ARNP, PSYMHCNS-BC
Psychiatric Nurse, Certified Spiritual Director

Dr. Eckrich has done a marvelous job of describing both the physiological and spiritual aspects of fear and anxiety. From a faith perspective, he identifies Christ and the forgiveness of sins as the source for healing, leading to a heart at peace. His professional and personal experiences substantiate his assertions and help the reader to relate to real-life applications. Since fear and anxiety are such important realities of the human experience, I recommend this book to all who seek to understand both their causes and cures.

Ted Kober
Founder and Senior Ambassador
Ambassadors of Reconciliation

Dr. Eckrich has dedicated his life to medicine, caring holistically for people in their times of illness, disease, and impending death. He understands the intimate connection that God intended between body and soul, which makes us who we are—humans created in the very image and likeness of God. It is also clear in his treatment of fear and anxiety that an important part of caring for people is providing helpful information about the effects of fear and anxiety on their personal wellbeing and the spiritual, psychological, and medical resources provided by God to help us live life to the fullest. Moreover, Dr. Eckrich understands his call as a Christian physician, providing a faithful witness to the love of God in Jesus Christ with a warm invitation to receive forgiveness, healing, and life to all who look to him for these blessings.

Rev. John Fale, BCC, AAPC Certified Fellow
Executive Director, Office of International Mission
Lutheran Church—Missouri Synod

As usual, Dr. Eckrich makes some fine distinctions and helps clergy, other ministers, and laity to navigate the complex and often dizzying world of stress, anxiety, fear, and guilt. With significant experience both in church circles and in the medical community, he not only translates higher-level psychology but also provides a framework for grafting sound psychological practices into Christian life and practice. This book is more than simply another psychological aid written for the educated clergyperson. It is an invaluable resource to help ministers to form healthier congregations while recognizing their own dysfunction. Dr. Eckrich encourages using the best of the psychological and theological traditions to work toward wholeness in Christ. He not only tells but also *shows* what it looks like to be thinking Christians—ones rooted deeply in grace and faith in the Lord's death and resurrection and ones who are willing to allow that grace to transform even the most broken, hidden parts of ourselves.

Fr. Dominic McManus, OP
Dominican Friar, Province of Albert the Great
Chicago, IL

For better or worse, fear and anxiety invade every facet of our lives. The real question is, "What do we do about it?" In this book Dr. Eckrich addresses the issues and the solutions. As a doctor, John offers practical suggestions for dealing with and overcoming the fears we face every day. From a Christian perspective he also offers faith-based solutions that simply eradicate incapacitating fear from our lives. These solutions allow us to tap into the healing power of Jesus Christ, offering us the peace of God that passes all understanding.

Ty Dodge
Chairman Emeritus, Realty South
Elder, Briarwood Presbyterian Church (PCA)
Lay Counselor, Bible Teacher

Through his work with Grace Place Ministries, Dr. Eckrich demonstrates his passion for bringing hope and healing to those who have answered the call to ministry. John helps us all understand how the lack of health—physical, spiritual, financial, emotional—negatively impacts our ability to live out our God-given vocation to the fullest. In this book John tackles the difficult issues of fear, anxiety, guilt, and shame from multiple perspectives as these emotions attack our wellbeing and serving. Physician, patient, cancer survivor, and gifted layman, John always brings us back to the perfect prescription for wellness and wholeness: the saving grace, through faith, that is ours in Jesus Christ!

James Sanft
President and CEO, Health and Benefit Plans
Concordia Plan Services, LCMS

Imagine three intersecting circles: gifted physician, devout man of God, and patient advocate. Dr. Eckrich is all three—ready, willing, and able to help us all navigate the cascade of dangers to peace. Drawing on all three perspectives, his brilliant narrative brings it all together to give readers an understanding of the many threats in our lives—anxiety, depression, and other mental health disorders. While we are blessed to have amazing psychotropic medications to treat these conditions, much work remains to be done to fully heal. Dr. Eckrich conveys the insights and faith to conquer these many challenges we all face, with Christ at the center.

Bill Mattson
Biopharma Executive

Follow Dr. Eckrich on his walk through fear, anxiety, guilt, and shame on the journey toward wellness. His walk includes his Gospel-based reflections born not only from theological and medical reflection but also, most importantly, from his own life's experience. This alone is worth the read. Add the lengthy appendix on the most common fear-based mental illnesses facing our culture and the reader has a small reference book as well.

Rev. Dr. Bruce Hartung
Professor of Pastoral Formation, Emeritus
Concordia Seminary, St. Louis, MO

Call it what you will, "it" creates fear, warranted or not. Ignore it, bury it, store it, or carry it—it will have its way with you until you apply Dr. Eckrich's hard-won wisdom from his professional and personal confrontations with this human phenomenon. He knows fear inside out and helps you name it, face it, and replace it with choices to conquer the beast and rest your weary soul. Free up your energy to live the life God, through Christ, intends.

Phyllis Wallace
Host, Syndicated Christian Women's Talk Show
Family Counselor, Author

Fear Anxiety and Wellness

JOURNEY TO A HEART AT PEACE

JOHN D. ECKRICH, M.D.

TENTH
POWER

Elgin, IL · Tyler, TX

TENTHPOWERPUBLISHING
www.tenthpowerpublishing.com

Softcover 978-1-938840-13-5

e-book 978-1-938840-14-2

10 9 8 7 6 5 4 3 2 1

To anxious Emmaus disciples on our Easter evening journey

TABLE OF CONTENTS

PREFACE

In a culture that has become more sophisticated, increasingly cynical, deeply anxious, and extraordinarily unhealthy, Dr. John Eckrich leads us on a comprehensive yet understandable journey through the role of fear in our lives. He brings a unique perspective from his training and many years of practice as a primary care and specialty physician, coupled with a view of fear and anxiety through the lens of Christian faith and theology. This book puts these two fields together in a creative and powerful way.

His focus is to open his readers to an understanding of Christ's invitation to all people to live with his peace in their hearts, rather than living with troubled and hardened spirits. He stays on target. He develops the medical and psychological understanding of fear as a constricting force that is accompanied by negative physical, emotional, and relational realities. Living in fear, anxiety, guilt, and shame has a devastating effect on a person's quality of life and intention of serving outside of themselves. It affects body, mind, and spirit. It challenges wellness.

The conclusion is simple: emotional/mental wellbeing is related to an open and transformable spirit. Emotional/mental ill-health is related to a spirit constricted and desensitized.

In an ingenious way, Dr. Eckrich integrates faith into the healing process. Living separated from God is the cause of basic anxiety, bringing awareness of personal vulnerability and eventual death. This is a *"me*-orientation" to life; you are "on your own." Protecting self is constricting and highly anxiety-producing!

Faith knows a restored spiritual connection with God, experiencing God's loving presence through Christ. This awareness of oneness with God by being restored to God's family through Christ's death and resurrection allows for a *"we*-orientation" to life. We are free to enjoy life, live abundantly, and serve the Creator and God's creation joyfully. Not having to protect self provides resilience and transformation. Faith is integral to the healing process by reducing anxiety and bringing peace.

In numerous personal and practical examples, Dr. Eckrich shows how faith works in real life to reduce fear and its effects. He takes us through the common dread that cancer and the fear of death bring, showing how the positive effects of community and one's relationship with God can help ease the reality of fear. He even shows a healthy way to deal with discord and conflict within one's personal family and faith community.

Throughout the book, he emphasizes that healing is most commonly a gradual process. It is best complemented by a coaching team: spiritual (pastors), physical (physicians) and emotional (counselors) mentors, and transformative life-practice changes. However, healing always flows from the fountain of our relationship with our Savior. He offers an exciting understanding of how being in God's Word, Baptism, the Lord's Supper, and confession and absolution help build faith and address the ravages of fear. Further, he suggests that spiritual discipline, particularly meditatively praying the Word of God, can encourage daily exercise of one's faith in concrete ways. This can make a substantial difference in developing healthy and resilient ways to handle all challenges of the body, mind, and spirit— the joyful as well as the distressful. The book is a dynamic discourse on the journey of wellness that God offers in Christ.

In the end, this Christian physician prays with all of God's people for hearts filled with peace.

Good job, Dr. John!

Rev. Dr. David J. Ludwig
Professor Emeritus, Department of Psychology
Ordained Clergy
Lenoir-Rhyne University
Hickory, NC

ACKNOWLEDGEMENTS

Fear permeates almost every aspect of life, especially when it comes to health issues. Therefore this book is based on the experiences of an immense pool of patients, including myself, who have faced fear and survived.

In the early phases of developing this story of hope for restoration to wellness, I asked several theologians and medical experts to review my thoughts regarding the Scriptural premises I have included, and the psychological features of mental illness. I wish to thank Rev. Dr. David Ludwig, noted pastor, psychologist, and author. David kindly has provided the preface for this book. Joining him is Dr. Mary Jacob, RN, a co-author with David of Christian Concepts for Care. Mary is also a certified spiritual director and psychiatric nurse. Additionally, I wish to thank Dr. Beverly Yahnke, executive director for Christian Counsel with DOXOLOGY and a licensed clinical psychologist, for her review of psychological strategies and care, particularly regarding the care of fear disorders and shame. I would like to recognize and thank Ted Kober, founder of Ambassadors of Reconciliation, for his thoughts regarding fear and anxiety in congregational and denominational conflicts.

From the medical/therapist perspective, I wish to thank Bruce Rau, M.D., a prominent psychiatrist from Angel Fire, New Mexico, and his wife, June Ryan, a psychiatric social worker and therapist.

Furthermore, I want to thank a group of pastoral counselors who have reviewed this material for content and accessibility. Included in this council are Rev. David Muench, director of ministerial care of Concordia Plan Services for the Lutheran Church—Missouri Synod, whose work in issues of shame I have included in this book; Rev. Dr. Bruce Hartung, author of Holding Up the Prophet's Hand and emeritus professor of pastoral formation at Concordia Seminary, St. Louis; Rev. Michael Frese, military chaplain and parish pastor of Redeemer Lutheran Church, Fort Wayne, Indiana, (awarded the Purple Heart for his service in Afghanistan). Additionally, I wish to thank Rev. Dr. Robert DeWetter, Episcopal priest and pastor of Snowmass Chapel, Snowmass, Colorado, and a distinguished clinical psychologist from UCLA.

I wish to thank Mark Zimmermann for his editing and encouragement.

Additionally, I wish to recognize and thank our great team at Grace Place Wellness Ministries in St. Louis. Grace Place Wellness offers retreats to church professionals to nurture vitality and joy in ministry by inspiring and equipping church workers to lead healthy lives. Our team includes Randy Fauser, President and CEO; Rev. Dr. Darrell Zimmerman, VP and Director of Programming; Beth McAnallen, Retreat and Technology Coordinator; and Kathy Evers, Office Manager.

As always, much appreciation goes to my wife of 40 years, Kathy, also a registered nurse, and my children, Chris, Molly, and Michael, for their patience and understanding.

Praise to God for his grace and constant faithfulness and bringing to you and me great Christian companions to continue this Emmaus journey, especially for the gift of Jesus.

John D. Eckrich, M.D.

INTRODUCTION

Robert is an athletic and energetic middle-aged gentleman who comes into my medical office. He hems and haws until he gets to the reason for his doctor visit, a spot on his arm. "Doc, do you think it's a melanoma?" he asks me hesitantly. I respond with a question of my own, "How long have you noticed that spot?" "My wife saw it three months ago, but I was so afraid to find out what it was!"

Sarah is a delightful 54-year-old woman and a tireless educator at the elementary school in our community. "I'm so embarrassed and so ashamed," she blurts out as tears fill her eyes. "I found this breast lump, and I just know it is cancer, just like my mother died of 15 years ago. And you know, Doc, I'm nearly her same age." She is ashen and literally wringing her hands.

Mary Claire is in her mid-60s, a wonderful, bright, and caring matriarch of a large family. Today, however, she looks disheveled, almost unrecognizable from the proper and prim, do-it-all woman who I recall from her last visit over two years ago. Mary Claire gazes longingly—and frankly I'm not sure she acknowledges me, her physician of 30 years. "Mom is having a tough time remembering certain things," her daughter says with trembling voice. "She's frightened, confused, and not eating or sleeping. "How long has she been like this?" I ask her daughter. "It's come on gradually over the last year," the daughter answers, a bit ashamedly. "I was so fearful that you might tell us Mom has, you know," she whispers, "Alzheimer's." Her daughter's eyes are filled with tears.

Jacob is a 21-year-old outstanding student at a prominent Big 10 university about to enter the workforce—he hopes! His parents, both patients of mine, urge him to see me on winter break, as they were struck by the level of fatigue and restlessness they had witnessed at Thanksgiving. He appears unfocused, disheveled, and obviously highly anxious. His parents were concerned about substance abuse. His opening words reveal something different. He quickly gets to the point. "Doctor John, I just worry about everything. Am I going to graduate on time? Am I going to get a job? Is my girlfriend going to dump me? Is my hair thinning? Is there something hidden inside me causing me to feel this way? I just feel out of control," and his gaze wanders as his voice drifts off into silence.

These are four fairly typical office visits in the day of most doctors. What they all have in common, along with a distressing sign or symptom, is the element of fear. That fear, often accompanied by devastating anxiety, substantially complicates and impedes their journey toward wellness.

In this book[1], I am asking you to pause with me to examine these most common emotions of fear and anxiety, and the feelings of guilt and shame that often accompany them. Discover with me how we might receive courage, hope, and energy to clarify and deal with our fears, bring calm to our lives, and wellness to our bodies, minds, and souls. I'll give you a preview. Christ brings us peace and Christ heals us, sometimes immediately, sometimes gradually—and surely, ultimately. Through Jesus Christ, as we walk the life-journey of illness, the fears that constrict our spirits and disrupt abundant living and serving can be replaced by a journey toward a wellness and peace that surpasses all understanding.

John D. Eckrich, M.D.

CHAPTER 1

FEAR DEFINED

P aul is a young father of two small children, a loving husband, a successful executive of a major business in our community, and a stalwart in our church. I fondly recall earlier days as he hopped to the front of our sanctuary for the children's message each Sunday, trying to corral two rambunctious young sons. He is not hopping today as he somberly sits in my exam room.

"Paul," I begin, "how's life? What brings you by this afternoon?" The conversation that follows is one I hear too frequently these days. "Doc, I'm beside myself with worry," and there are clearly tears beginning to form at the edges of his eyes. "I'm not sure where to start," and his voice trails off into intense sobs; I now detect the faint odor of alcohol on his breath. "Everything is collapsing; my health, my marriage, my job, my friends, everything. The board is going after me; it's not my fault that business is tanking! I hate them all and I'm going to make them pay for the way they're treating me!" he stammers. "I can't sleep, I've lost 15 pounds...no appetite...I'm fighting with my wife and screaming at my babies..." and his thoughts disintegrate into further tears. "I'm losin' it, Doc, I'm losin' it."

Paul is consumed by fear. And Paul has allowed fear to cascade down a turbulent and destructive torrent of additional emotions, including intense anxiety with accompanying physical signs and symptoms. He expresses guilt, bitterness, shame, and even malice toward his bosses. He is trying to cope, even using substances (alcohol) to try to self-medicate and calm his emotions; but at the fountainhead of this turmoil is *fear.*

> *"If God is for us, who can be against us? He who did not spare his own Son, but gave him up for us all—how will he not also, along with him, graciously give us all things?...No, in all these things we are more than conquerors through him who loved us. For I am convinced that neither death nor life, neither angels nor demons, neither the present nor the future, nor any powers, neither height nor depth, nor anything else in all creation, will be able to separate us from the love of God that is in Christ Jesus our Lord." (Romans 8:31-39)*

Fear is one of the most common emotions shared by all of creation since the *Fall* of humanity. It deeply can influence all parts of our wellbeing: body, mind, and spirit. It is part of every visit made to a physician's office, and is so often present in the conversations that fill pastors' studies, teachers' classrooms, financial advisers' consultations, visits to the auto repair shop, and the day-to-day communications in every home and hut across this planet. And fear is deeply embedded in the self-talk we each have within us.

In this book we want to not only talk about fear but also try to understand it. We want to look at this emotion, and the linked chain of additional emotions that often devastatingly flow from it, particularly anxiety. We want to see how they affect our wellness journey. Our hope is to find some pathways, especially from a Christian perspective, to seek comfort, healing, wellness, and peace through our Lord.

We will approach this task using a medical, behavioral, and most importantly, a Scripturally based, faith-focused lens to examine fear and its associated emotions. With each perspective, our goal is to provide a clarity of understanding and comprehensive *prescriptions* for facing these most common emotions, as well as encouragement and empowerment on our wellness journey.

Fear

First off, let's define fear. Fear can be defined as a feeling brought about by a real and immediate threat or danger that brings about physical, metabolic (body chemistry), or behavioral changes in the way we function. The feeling is one of apprehension, nervousness, and hyper-alertness. You've been fearful. You know the feeling! Even Wikipedia describes fear as an "appropriate cognitive[1] and emotional response to a perceived threat and is related to the specific behaviors of fight-or-flight response." These physical changes lead to a redirected behavior that either causes us to confront or flee from the danger, and that is exactly what we call the "fight-or-flight" response, or more simply the *fear response.*

Fear arises in humans because of a *perception* of danger, either a specific stimulus or threat, or even the *expectation* of a future threat that we would anticipate being a risk to body or life itself.

Words for fear are in virtually every tongue from the ancient dialects, to Scriptural writings, to the Romance languages, to modern vernacular. Writings and descriptions of fear extend as far back as Aristotle in Western literature, and centuries before in Eastern writings and thought. Fear appears to be the most universal and consistent response to real or perceived danger of all inhabitants of the earth. This response to danger not only crosses human cultures but even exists among the higher animals. Across cultures and species, the primary fear of all creatures is pain or death, both implying separation or loss. All the stimuli causing fear are unpleasant.

The threat of death, pain, or loss can be real or imagined. *Most often,* fear is proximity focused, immediate, generally short-term, and usually has a singular focus.

Some definitions of fear, including those in the medical/psychological literature, do get muddied by including fear of something dangerous, painful, or unknown that *might* happen (which I will discuss as we look at the term *anxiety*), but most clinical therapists tend to reserve the use of this word, fear, for being afraid of something more immediately threatening.

Let me share a brief and common example. We may discover a new physical symptom, like an unusual headache, and our worry and fright continue until we have the energy and determination to achieve a proper diagnosis—sinus headache! Once we have clarity, and receive appropriate therapy, the fear aspect of this symptom generally resolves, and we avoid moving that fear into something more ominous to our health—that is moving down an emotional chain reaction into *anxiety*.

CHAPTER 2

THE LINKED CHAIN OF FEAR—ANXIETY, GUILT, SHAME

B arry awoke one sunny morning, almost tumbling out of his bed due to the sudden onset of dizziness, or medically what we might call *vertigo*. This spinning sensation lasted most of the morning, and seemed to lessen by early afternoon. He did notice, when he bent down to get something in the cupboard, upon standing he thought he was tilting around like riding on a tilt-a-whirl.

Although less intense, the sensation seemed to persist for the next several weeks. Of course, Barry looked on Wikipedia, WebMD, and other sites, always convincing himself that this was temporary, due to too much coffee, or sugar, or whatever, and that the serious illnesses (strokes, brain cancer, others) listed on the websites applied to *others*, but not to him.

However, the vertigo persisted. As the dizziness continued, his worry and rumination increased. He found himself anxiously awakening a few hours after going to bed and unable to fall asleep again. He lost his taste for food, and for him, that was almost an unimaginable happening. He even noticed his hands trembling, which of course drove him back to the Internet, where he was now thoroughly convinced he had an enormous malignancy growing right between his eyes. Furthermore, he developed a cold that he just couldn't shake.

Finally, his dear wife drew a line in the sand. "Sit down with me here at the kitchen table. Take my hand and we're just going to pray about this crazy dizziness." They prayed.

"Now, you are going to see Dr. Eckrich tomorrow. I made the appointment for 10:00 in the morning. Be there or be square, Honey!"

> *"Do not be anxious about anything, but in every*
> *situation, by prayer and petition, with thanksgiving,*
> *present your requests to God. And the peace of God, which*
> *transcends all understanding, will guard your hearts*
> *and your minds in Christ Jesus." (Philippians 4:6-7)*

Although fear is seen as short-term and more singularly focused in most cases, what is long-term is the linked chain of fear, which includes the other linked emotions that are integrally connected to this most common reaction to stress.

After fear, the next link in the chain is *anxiety*. Anxiety is defined as a long-acting, generally future-focused response (often not immediately or sensory experienced), broadly resulting from a more diffuse threat, and producing excessive caution that can interfere with constructive coping, or even healing. Well-known mental health therapist David Barlow defines anxiety as "a future-oriented mood state in which one is ready or prepared to attempt to cope with upcoming negative events." There is, he says, "a distinction between future and present dangers which divides anxiety from fear."[2]

What was initially fear falls tumbling down the emotional waterfall into a more pathological (illness-producing) emotion, anxiety, by becoming perpetual, excessive, exaggerated, and projected into an uncertain future. Our fear can become self-isolating and can completely consume every moment of life. In anxiety, that initial fear begins to consume our very *spirit* or *soul.*

Although both fear and anxiety can be accompanied by similar physical effects of fight-or-flight, anxiety tends to interfere excessively with coping mechanisms through adversely altering sleep, cardiovascular and gastrointestinal function, and immunity. It can even cause repetitive motor activity, much of which is due to repeated release of stress hormones like cortisol, adrenaline, and oxytocin. In one way or another, the common denominator of the cognitive effects of fear and anxiety tends to be the apprehension of suffering loss, pain, or death from the danger.

While fear is common to all creatures, human and animal, in response to such things as loud or unexpected noises and threats of imminent harm, pain, or death, anxieties more often are learned from previous exposure to the frightening stimuli with accompanying automated emotional and physical reactions. We often pair objects or events with threatening experiences, and then normally nonthreatening objects or circumstances can produce the same response—anxiety. Please consult the appendix to follow the use of this word *anxiety* from a historical perspective as it may reflect the way we see anxiety described in the various translations of the Scriptures and in modern medical literature, particularly in the Diagnostic and Statistical Manual of Mental Disorders (DSM-5).

The word itself, *anxiety,* stems directly from the Latin *angor,* and the verb *ango*, which means to *constrict*, highly similar to the German and other central European languages' word *angst*. Even in Biblical Hebrew, for example, we see Job expressing his anguish (anxiety) in Job 7:10 with the Hebrew expression "the narrowness [*tsar*] of my spirit."

We see this concept of *anguish* or *constriction* of the spirit repeatedly associated with the worry and anxiety accompanying many physical and emotional disorders up to this very day. I believe it is appropriate to say that a spirit that is not just *constricted* but also *numb or desensitized, closed,* and *non-transformable* is a spirit filled with anxiety. On the other hand, a spirit that is open and transformable is more likely at peace and well.

Guilt

Another link in the emotional chain reaction of fear is guilt, which is defined as "sorrow for what we have done." A quick look into the *American Heritage Medical Dictionary* (2007) uses a legal sense in terminology for guilt, but correlates closely with the Biblical sense of responsibility for the commission of an offense or act, moral or legal, and culpability for the offense. Medically, guilt extends to responsibility for a mistake, whether intentional or unintentional. It appears to come from the Old English word *gylt,* meaning delinquency. In psychological thought it is a sad or remorseful feeling caused by tension between the ego[3] and superego [4] when one falls below the standard one sets for oneself or the standard set by others. It implies an awareness of having done something wrong. In other words, there is a recognition of not living up to a legal or moral law.

More simply stated, *guilt* means I did something bad of my own volition. Therefore the healing of that guilt needs to include apologizing (confessing and showing sorrow, hopefully leading to forgiveness), making amends if possible, and then changing our behavior so that we don't repeat the offense. Guilt can be a *positive* influence on our behavior; it is helpful; it can move us in the right direction.

Chronic depression, chronic anxiety disorders, and obsessive-compulsive behavior may all result when people are unable to move past their guilt. People carrying chronic guilt may find it impossible to sustain relationships. Medical treatment involves guided talk or mindfulness therapy, and often includes the involvement of the entire person's family to work through the feelings of guilt.

Also, there can be a sense of *embarrassment* associated with guilt. The embarrassment associated with guilt generally comes about externally; it is embarrassment brought about by a societal reaction to one's misbehavior. In fact there are societies in which guilt greatly defines the moral and legal standards of the culture. The United States is such a society; a person may do something wrong, but apologizing and making amends within this guilt-culture can erase the blot on one's character. Frankly, Judaism and Christianity both share a guilt culture, where the conscience urges one to atone for their misdeeds.

Shame

Far more toxic in the linked chain of fear is shame. Shame moves a step beyond remorse for what one has done in error, and adds the dimension of owning that error as a definition of who we are as a flawed human being.

Shame means that not only what we have done is bad, but that *we are bad!* Therefore when we are ashamed by our human nature we tend to act out in a way to protect ourselves. So we blame others. We remember Adam and Eve's initial response to their Creator: blame each other and blame the serpent. Our apologies can be insincere or disingenuous. We tend to hide or isolate ourselves from our accusers and from the fear and anxiety induced by the recognition of our misdeeds by ourselves or others. Shame is a self-destructive behavior, and shame erodes the part of us that believes we can change our behavior and not err again. In this aspect of shame we see a strong correlation with the addiction cycle, self-harm, or harm inflicted on others. Additionally, depression, eating disorders, aggressive and violent behavior, and even bullying can flow from shame. Shame generally produces negative outcomes.

Shame is extremely painful and filled with fear. All humans experience shame, except for sociopaths, who are unable to feel empathy. We are fearful of talking about our shame, and the less we talk about it, the more it takes control of our lives. We own our shame; we feel we deserve it.

Medically, and psychiatrically, shame often originates from an emotional state beginning in childhood, filled with self-reproach. It is a sense of not just personal failure, but a personal fundamental flaw. It may begin with a spilled glass of milk. If the parent is angry and scolds but then quickly forgives and demonstrates love, the guilt and shame are short-lived and the shame is diffused. However, if the parental response to spilling the milk includes not just rejection of the behavior but rejection of the child, the shame becomes internalized and can become chronic and toxic. The embarrassment associated with shame can be experienced societally, as with guilt, but also can be experienced *secretly*, which can be far more destructive. It is, in a true sense, *hiding*. It is the secrecy of this emotion that is so toxic, but that also gives us a specific tool with which to provide healing.

In shame cultures, like those of ancient Greece and Japan, there is great emphasis on what *others* think of you. In shame cultures, when you transgress you lose respect; you are disgraced. The only way to reenter the good graces of family or society in shame cultures is to suffer through the passage of time, even if you do apologize or try to make amends.

Another particularly destructive aspect of shame is that, unlike other primary emotions, shame lacks a channel for discharging its destructive energy. For example, when we are angry, we can shout or lash out. When we are sad, we can cry. But shame remains internal, and can intensify without an outlet for release. With shame the outlet itself becomes destructive through dissociating, lashing out, or self-destructive behavior such as the use of illicit drugs, sexual promiscuity, or other dangerous activity.

Men and women experience shame somewhat differently. Rev. David Muench, a pastoral counselor and psychologist who is a leader in the Christian community on guilt and shame among church professionals, suggests that men are *strength-oriented*. When men experience shame, it means they have failed to perform tasks at work or within the family setting. Shame equals failure. Here again, shame means you are wrong, not just doing something in the wrong manner, but personally wrong, defective, or weak. Men fear being criticized or laughed at. This leads to men shutting down emotionally or getting angry, becoming judgmental or vindictive, or developing malice (a desire to harm someone else). A significant amount of Dr. Muench's work is based on the shame research accomplished by Dr. Brené Brown and reported in her seminal work, *I Thought It Was Just Me (But It Isn't): Making the Journey from "What Will People Think?" to "I Am Enough."*

On the other hand, particularly in our culture, Rev. Muench describes women experiencing shame in a societal and comparative context. Just view any popular magazine, TV show, or Facebook posting and you will see the endless comparisons of hair, beauty, body composition, child-rearing effectiveness, and innumerable other attributes with which we judge each other and ourselves. Women can feel ashamed if they don't meet the mark among their peers.

Rev. Muench also describes another format for shame in women as "mother shame." This displays itself in one of three variations of shame: "soon enough," "often enough," or "well enough." This aspect of shame is often displayed in "do-it-all" women who might choose to wait to bear children later in life due to career choices (soon enough). Second, statements to mothers of, "Oh, are you not able to have more children?" or, "You're not quitting already, are you?" are examples of the "often enough" shame placed on women by our culture. The "well enough" shame is applied to women of all ages regarding their child-rearing styles or effectiveness. Women are judged, mostly by other women, on the way their children behave or follow instruction in the grocery store, school, or church. These types of criticisms of mothers can produce extraordinary anxiety and shame in women.

Behaviorally, we all may display our shame in a variety of actions. We might become self-destructive, channeling our shame inwardly. Or we might appear arrogant or even narcissistic (meaning possessing excessive vanity or self-admiration) and avoid relationships in an attempt to cover up a deep sense of shame. Finally, as seen most often in men, we might become aggressive, transferring our shame onto others by acting out angrily toward them.

I will discuss suggestions for the care and treatment of shame from a Christian spiritual viewpoint, but let me just note here that shame is extraordinarily difficult, if not impossible, to *self-treat*. I believe significant shame requires the help of professionally trained counselors who can help create a safe environment for therapy, and that includes the care of pastoral guidance, as shame has a deeply seated spiritual element. The most effective therapeutic counseling work begins with a recognition in the *counselor* that shame is universal and the therapist needs to have a solid recognition of their *own* shame. Sharing personal vulnerability, empathy, and compassion as a therapist can be extremely helpful to the one you counsel or pastor.

Second, the therapist will help the counseled to "break the code of secrecy and silence" surrounding and underlying the shame. The counselor guides the shamed person into openly discussing the various feelings surrounding their emotions, and helps the shamed recognize how they might be acting the shame out in daily behavior.

Third, the therapist can help the individual restore what Rev. Muench and other therapists call *shame resilience* through a reacceptance of self-worth. The therapist helps the individual regain their *rights,* understand their *worth* to themselves, to their family, or to their community.

Two other related emotional responses to our misbehavior can be *humiliation* and *embarrassment.* Humiliation comes as a result of being criticized or belittled, but in the setting where we don't feel the criticism is deserved. *Humiliation* is negative, unearned, or undeserved from *our* perspective. *Embarrassment* carries less emotional energy or charge. It is more fleeting, and we feel as if we can laugh at ourselves over our behavior (laugh-with-me rather than laugh-at-me). Embarrassment has a time-limited effect on us; it will pass on without indefinitely defining us in the eyes of others.

Hopefully these descriptions of characteristics and interrelationships between fear, anxiety, guilt, and shame can provide greater understanding of these emotional responses, and help us recognize the powerful and spiraling destruction of fear and anxiety. More importantly, these understandings may provide impetus for us to seek healing for our emotional and relational suffering earlier rather than later.

Permit me a moment to share a linked chain of fear from my own experience. One of the great and legendary stories among my children involves what I now realize is the linked chain reaction of fear. It is a *favorite* holiday story. I'm guessing that you have your own version of this tale if you are a parent, but here's mine.

It was the evening of Christmas Day in the 1990s when we gathered as a family, including our three teenage children and several teenage nieces and nephews. Up to this point I remember feeling my kids and their cousins were a pretty good bunch (and, frankly, I still do!). On occasion, there were a few behavioral issues typical or at least appropriate for their respective ages.

The entire extended family was over for Christmas supper with lots of good food, drink, and conversation. Mid-evening, I noticed an absence of the teenagers in the main gathering room in our home but just suspected they were out in other parts of the house.

At about 11:30 P.M., the teen crew came in quietly, sheepishly, and covered knee-deep in mud! There was a different sense of fear pervading the space between the parents and the teenagers in our family room. We, as parents, were *anxious* and projecting what might have led to the great accumulation of mud everywhere. I also can assure you, from the looks on five teens' faces, that they had both fear and anxiety, and anticipated a significant punishment for the cause of why they were covered in mud.

It turns out that they had spent the last three hours trying to extricate my son's Jeep Wrangler from a sloppy, muddy, and icy bog winding around a neighborhood under construction. They had figured it would be cool to zip around the empty lots, but they got stuck immediately and finally had to get a tow truck to rescue them.

Yes, they had *high anxiety*. They had coupled *fear* of their parents' displeasure and immediate consequences of that displeasure with a very unpleasant, guilty, shameful *anxiety* that they had changed the relationship, and the *spiritual* trust of our family for the future. They were *guilty* of disobedience, and, indeed, I think *ashamed*. These teens chose to neglect, "Children, obey your parents in the Lord, for this is right." "Honor your father and mother," which is the first commandment with a promise, "that it may go well with you and that you many enjoy long life on the earth." (Ephesians 6:1-3, Deuteronomy 5:16, Exodus 20:12) My dear kids substituted obedience for *be not just afraid, but be very anxious, because this may not go so well with you in the future*. Their fear was couched in guilt of potential punishment and shame. It was a fear where your "rights" can be taken from you, not just temporarily, but altered well into the future. For me that experience is a prime example of the linked chain of fear and its cascade of consequences!

CHAPTER 3

DEFINING THE JOURNEY TOWARD WELLNESS

The title and subject of this book include the concept of *wellness*. *Wellness* is a popular topic in our 21st-century culture and it has been the desire of God for creation as first recorded in the book of Genesis in the Bible. Before drilling down further into those emotional and relational stresses that consume the discussion at hand—fear, anxiety, guilt, and shame—let me provide a reminder of what I mean by *wellness* from the perspective of a physician who is Christian. Wellness is the focus of my first book in this series entitled *Vocation and Wellness: Renew Your Energy for Christian Living.* It's available at www.amazon.com or www.graceplacewellness.org.

Wellness, as defined in *Vocation and Wellness,* is a "grace-gift of God in Christ, inviting us to consciously steward body, mind, spirit, vocation, and resources to God's glory and service with vitality and joy." The Christian Wellness Wheel I refer to in that book, and that is increasingly seen in the writings of Christian health literature, serves as a helpful model to understand and pursue our wellness journey. A reproduction of that Wheel is found on the back page of this book.

Galatians 5:22-23, the *fruit of the Spirit,* and St. Paul's book to the Christians at Ephesus, Ephesians 4:1-32, stand as Scriptural background to discuss wellness on Grace Place[5] Wellness Retreats (GPW). These are held around the world to encourage a wellness journey in Christ for professional church workers and laity alike. Therefore I will use the *wellness characteristics* outlined by St. Paul in both Ephesians and Galatians for our discussion here.

> *"But the fruit of the Spirit is love, joy, peace,*
> *forbearance (patience), kindness, goodness,*
> *faithfulness, gentleness, and self-control. Against such*
> *things there is no law." (Galatians 5:22-23)*

Correlating to the Christian Wellness Wheel as used in GPW programming, Rev. Dr. Darrell Zimmerman, Vice President of Programming for GPW, has described the following *markers* to guide a discussion of wellness in Christian life and vocation, utilizing a Galatians 5:22-23 and Ephesians 4:1-32 perspective:

- Baptismal Wellbeing: As I grow in God's grace of Baptismal LOVE, I am finding joy in my IDENTITY as a new creation in Christ. (the center of the Wellness Wheel)

- Spiritual Wellbeing: As I grow in God's grace of Spiritual GOODNESS, I am finding joy in RECEPTIVITY to God's gifts, maturing and growing in Christ. (the outer all-encompassing envelope of the Wellness Wheel)

- Relational Wellbeing: As I grow in God's grace of Relational PATIENCE, I am finding joy in my UNITY in Christ with spouse, personal family, and faith family.

- Intellectual Wellbeing: As I grow in God's grace of Intellectual KINDNESS, I am finding joy in CURIOSITY, listening and speaking in a beneficial way.

Christian Wellness Wheel
FRUIT OF THE SPIRIT · GALATIANS 5:22-23

- Emotional Wellbeing: As I grow in God's grace of Emotional PEACE, I am finding joy in HARMONY with others by the healing power of forgiveness. *You will note here how the themes of peace, harmony, and forgiveness are challenged and disrupted in fear, anxiety, guilt, and shame discussed in the core of this book.*

- Vocational Wellbeing: As I grow in God's grace of Vocational GENTLENESS, I am finding joy in HUMILITY as I serve through my calling and gifts.

- Physical Wellbeing: As I grow in God's grace of Physical SELF-CONTROL, I am finding joy in the VITALITY that flows from practicing healthy choices.

- Financial Wellbeing: As I grow in God's grace of Financial FAITHFULNESS, I am finding joy in GENEROSITY, sharing with others as I have been blessed.

With the additional foundation of these definitions of *wellness*, let us now delve deeper into the medical, behavioral, Biblical, and faith-based concepts of the distress brought about by emotional, mental, and relational disorder on our earthly journey.

CHAPTER 4

FEAR AND ANXIETY FROM A MEDICAL/ BEHAVIORAL PERSPECTIVE

Roberta is a delightful middle-aged social worker in our community's family services division. She comes in for her yearly physical and blood work, but she looks to me like she has found the 20 or so pounds she had spent the last several years discarding. She's known as a kind, calming influence to so many families in crisis in our region, although I don't know a lot about her own personal family circumstances.

"Roberta, I see you don't have much new to report on your history and physical pre-visit sheet. But I noticed nurse Betty found you to be fitting a bit more tightly around the waistband; looks like you've gained back about 20 pounds. Your heart rate is up, blood pressure is raised nearly 15 points, and your lab shows your fasting blood sugar and cholesterol are both at dangerous levels. I see your Mom had diabetes. Anything going on I should be aware of?"

Wow, it is like I am opening the floodgates on a pent-up emotional river. Here come the tears, accompanied by a tome of her marital discord, her teenagers' struggles with drugs, and a long-standing and a hurtful episode with her sister. To top that off, she is afraid of losing her job with the local government's recent funding proposal going down to defeat in the last election. Fear upon fear; anxiety upon anxiety.

> *"So we say with confidence, 'The Lord is my helper; I will not be afraid. What can mere mortals do to me?'" (Hebrews 13:6)*

When we talk about fear from a medical perspective, it is helpful for us to remember that many physicians, therapists, and even the general public use the words *fear* and *anxiety* interchangeably. Part of this semantic and definitional double-talk is that fear and anxiety are tightly interrelated, not just in their conceptual origin, but also in how they affect the human body, intellect, and feelings. This is due to the identical triggering of the *stress or fear response* in the human *nervous, cardiovascular, and gastrointestinal systems* with both fear and anxiety. The body releases cells, enzymes, hormones, and biochemical compounds that interact in complex regulation of our nervous, cardiovascular, digestive, and immune systems.

The medical field understands that fear is a natural response to stressful stimuli and positively may help us avoid harm, and then return our body to homeostasis, or baseline. But when our fear turns into pathological (illness-producing) anxiety, it does so by becoming all-consuming, and offsetting of our ability to balance, cope, or recover effectively after responding to real or perceived danger. Having traveled down that linked emotional chain from fear to anxiety, interventional medical and psychological treatment may be needed to get us balanced.

Simple fear and associated worry and anxiety can more fully deteriorate our ability to be resilient to stress. When this stress/fear response happens repeatedly, without having been necessarily stimulated by logically threatening danger (and therefore continuously bathing the body with stress chemicals and hormones), we call it an *anxiety disorder*. One example of this might be what therapists would call a generalized anxiety disorder

(GAD). People with GAD tend to expect disaster everywhere and they just can't stop worrying about their health, family, money, work, or school. The worry is excessive for the particular situation. Everyday living is filled with dread and fear for them. If left untreated, the anxiety begins to interfere with their jobs, their schoolwork, their social activities, and their relationships. To learn more about GAD, please consult the appendix.

There are other anxiety disorders. When a fear response is extreme, or disproportionate to the potential danger, irrational, or obsessive, we apply the medical term *phobia* to that anxiety. People with a phobia do everything they can to avoid what they see as a particularly anxiety-producing object, activity, or situation. Anxiety is often a learned reaction. We've been in similar dangerous circumstances before, and we understand how those dangers might have affected us in the past. For example, someone might have a fear of anything white and fluffy. Their fear response began when they were startled by the sudden hop of a tiny Easter bunny as a very young child. However, they transfer that fear to white cotton candy, or a tuft of white cotton at the art table at school, or a white woolen sweater that they avoid wearing. Therefore their fear can be appropriate to a specific stimulus or situation, or become inappropriate if the threat is only imagined, or future-projected, or associated with a previous learned experience but is inappropriate for a current, non-harmful stimulus. Additionally, we can obsess or ruminate over our fear of that object. These phobias can extend to a social situation (social anxiety disorder) or to being removed from a parent or close friend (separation anxiety disorder). To learn more about phobias, please consult the appendix.

Other common anxiety-related disorders resulting from an exaggerated response to fear might include panic attacks, obsessive-compulsive disorder (OCD), post-traumatic stress disorder (PTSD or PTS), agoraphobia, anxiety disorder due to a medical condition, selective mutism, separation anxiety disorder (in childhood), substance-induced anxiety disorder, and other unspecified anxiety disorders. These illnesses all have anxiety as their root cause and you can examine the appendix for full descriptions and effective therapies for all of them.

It is also important to understand that fear and anxiety are two of only a few primary emotions recognized by physicians as common to all of us. Some of the other emotional responses include sadness, fright, joy, panic, and anger. As with the anxiety disorders, these emotions probably also are tied closely to structures at the base of our brain called the limbic system, particularly to groups of neural tissue called the amygdala and the hippocampus. These central brain tissues are closely associated with the body's hypothalamus, pituitary, and adrenal tissues, also called the HPA-axis. The HPA-axis is triggered in all of us when we are fearful or anxious.

Fear and Anxiety Brain Structures and Interactions

Let us turn first in the brain to the amygdala. The amygdala is made up of two almond-shaped groups of nuclei located deeply and medially within the temporal lobes of the brain. Please refer to the diagram of the HPA-axis in the appendix under Neurochemistry of Stress, Fear, and Anxiety. These little almonds of complex brain tissue occur in humans and other animals. The amygdala seems to have a primary role in the processing of memory, decision-making, and many emotional reactions. Located near the amygdala is the hippocampus, also implicated in the processing of emotional memory. Both the amygdala and the hippocampus are closely wired to the HPA-axis mentioned above. With such tight connections between the limbic system and the HPA-axis you can easily understand how memory-induced learning, particularly of threatening events, can cause us to physically respond with hyper-alertness, nervousness, crying, stuttering, altered sleep patterns, shallow breathing, loss of appetite, and tension throughout our being.

Fear and anxiety can be tied to a variety of more intensive mental health disorders and behavioral concerns. Beyond anxiety disorders, which have also been called *neuroses*, we recognize people who become delusional or have psychotic hallucinations, or *psychoses,* and they also experience very high levels of fear and anxiety. We commonly say psychotic patients are "out of touch with reality." Psychotic patients have fear integral to their more serious clinical mental health illnesses such as paranoia, clinical depression, bipolar disorder, and schizophrenia. Again, look to the appendix for further definitions of some of these illnesses.

Medically, we know there may be a genetic or inherited component to anxiety disorders. There are "anxious" families and there may be specific gene sites within our chromosomes (the genetic blueprints in each cell) correlated with some anxiety disorders.

Many medical conditions can spawn anxiety directly or indirectly, particularly with chronic diseases. Substance abuse (illicit drugs and alcohol) of all kinds can exacerbate anxiety either from excessive use, or from withdrawal from these agents. Certain chemicals, like benzene and other toxins, might produce anxiety.

Finally, physicians and therapists understand that poor coping skills, usually learned and often part of family dynamics, can be linked to a variety of anxiety disorders. Cognitive distortion and unhealthy thought, like always thinking the worst possible scenario will happen, can lead to anxiety disorders.

Neurochemistry of Stress, Fear, and Anxiety

When stressed, our human body responds through the aforementioned *HPA-axis* (hypothalamic-pituitary-adrenal interactive organs) and the *SNS* (sympathetic nervous system). These are homeostatic (regulatory and balancing) systems between our brain and our body's cells that make up what we might call the *stress system.* There is a cascade of hormones and chemicals (neurotransmitters, neuroreceptor-proteins, and up- and down-regulating secretions) released within this stress system, all highly interactive with each other. We are learning more each day about the way these hormones affect our health or ill-health. What we do understand regarding our fears and anxieties is that excessive, prolonged, or inadequate regulation of this stress response system can have substantial adverse health consequences. For those interested in the remarkable advancements in the neurochemistry of fear and anxiety, please seek information in the appendix under Neurochemistry of Stress, Fear, and Anxiety.

We also understand that the feedback system that controls how much and how long the HPA-axis is activated can be affected by the chronic stimulation of stress and anxiety.

It is valuable to note, too, that people suffering long-term anxiety often tend to have substantial sleep disorders and might utilize coffee, alcohol, or other stimulants and suppressants to self-medicate. There are fascinating studies showing that caffeine and alcohol increase cortisol production (a steroid hormone produced under stress by the HPA-axis), as does sleep deprivation. Think about your student days when you were fearful about a final exam, stayed up all night studying by consuming volumes of coffee, and then celebrated the end of finals with an evening of pizza and beer. That was the perfect *cortisol storm*! No wonder students are often overly anxious and get sick after finals week.

Behavioral Interactions

As we develop physically and emotionally, we do so in a healthy fashion when we grow within secure relationships with others. When we feel secure we are much more capable of dealing with stress, fear, and anxiety. Our security bonds with others become stronger when we have repeated stresses or fears that are then relieved by turning to a secure relationship. Psychologists call this a *distress-relief dynamic*. Please allow me to digress for just a moment and to interject a note here for us as Christians; the strength of this bond is dependent on the consistent nature of those with whom we are attached. If our attachment is to one who is available, attentive, and responsive, our fears and anxieties are calmed. We know as Christians that our bond is with God through Christ. God is unchanging. God loves us unconditionally in Jesus Christ despite the continual stress and fear of sin. We have faith that God always answers our prayers, according to God's will, not our own; but God always answers us.

And *God always heals*. Sometimes God heals *immediately*, such as in a miracle. As a physician I believe I have seen miracles of healing—immediate and scientifically unexplainable. Most often, however, God heals through a *process* of healing; God heals *gradually*. Healing may not occur immediately; it may take surgery, medications, radiation therapy, setbacks, and time. Sometimes it is challenging to see this healing process amid human suffering. Finally, God *always* heals us *ultimately*. God takes us to eternity in Jesus. When we die in Christ, God changes us from ones limited by our physical bodies (perishable) to ones of a spiritual nature (imperishable). (1 Corinthians 15:35-58) The families of sick people, and patients themselves when facing imminent death from cancer or heart disease, may question whether their faith is strong enough. They wonder whether God is inconsistently listening to their pleas when things don't appear to be headed toward temporal healing. Yet for many people in the distress of illness the only relief of their suffering may be for God to bring them into eternity. God is the only one who can relieve their ills. God heals them ultimately and brings them to the home Jesus is preparing for them forever. Our faith, strengthened and preserved by the Holy Spirit, assures us of God's consistent, unconditional, and unending listening and love as well as the ultimate healing through Christ.

As a physician I've been asked this question many times: "Why is this happening to me?" My only response, in faith, is to listen, share a time of compassionate understanding and sometimes the empathy of frustration and anger, and finally, share God's Word in prayer: "And we know that in all things God works for the good of those who love him, who have been called according to his purpose." (Romans 8:28) This is the comfort of Jesus attaching himself to us, transforming us in our Baptism and affirmation of faith.

Conversely, if we attach ourselves to figures who are unavailable, inattentive, unresponsive, and inconsistent, we may look for security elsewhere, perhaps within ourselves, leading to severely negative self-talk, or in other venues that lead to self-harm such as addictions.

And most interestingly, when we are threatened by any means, we are motivated to form attachments. Could it be, again as Christians, that we know that God does not wish us harm, but is present amid the dangers of this world, to welcome and gather us children, to carry us through the troubles of this life, to "lift us on eagle's wings"? I don't mean that to be platitudinous or trite; I say it as one who has been lifted on those very wings.

Similarly, we know that threatening, painful, or separating events can motivate us toward relationships within a group, again, as faith-filled Christians within God's family. We face the threat of pain or death far more healthily when we affiliate with our social and faith family.

Recent medical research has even suggested that the neuropeptide oxytocin is released in our system in response to dangerous stimuli. Oxytocin causes us to move to seek friendship, the so-called "tend and befriend" hypothesis.

Remember, we talked about the sympathetic nervous system and the HPA-axis a bit earlier as biochemical descriptions of the two major ways we respond to stress and fear. There is an additional wealth of scientific literature that suggests that family and good social support systems reduce the load on the sympathetic nervous system and substantially boost our immune function during times of fear.

One additional note from behavioral science and psychology: There is another category of neuropeptides we produce in our system called *endogenous opioids*, and these neuropeptides are released in stress-reducing relationships. We know from studying people who are addicted to opiates that the opiates produce euphoria, satiation, and wellbeing, as well as substantially reduce our sensitivity to both physical and emotional pain. Our endogenous opioids seem to also draw us into relationships of dependency, which if withdrawn can mirror the grief process. Again, the suggestion is that if we are drawn into loving relationships, our stress, fear, and anxiety are diminished.

There is great hope that as we further discover ways to accurately measure some of these hormones and complex protein structures in the blood, urine, and other tissues that we can continue to develop more successful armaments to aid in the healing of many mental illnesses. New treatments may complement what we know are essential, including spiritual care, diet (more veggies/decreased sweets/good breakfast/high unrefined fiber), good monitoring of blood sugars, adequate sleep and rest, exercise, and weight control.

CHAPTER 5

FEAR AND ANXIETY FROM A BIBLICAL PERSPECTIVE

We have examined the medical, behavioral, and biochemical understandings and definitions for fear and the linked chain of fear. Undoubtedly and definitively, the best place for a follower of Christ to seek an understanding of fear and its linked chain reactions is to clarify what these human responses mean for our body, mind, and spirit in God's holy Word.

Could there be any examples from the Bible regarding stories of fear? The word *fear* seems to be a topic occurring more than 500 times in the Scriptures; I would think that it is an important topic!

Remember Esau and Jacob, sort of the poster boys for family dysfunction! Esau is born first, but not without a fight as his twin brother Jacob grabs Esau's heel coming out the womb to try to gather the first blessing of their father, Isaac. The boys bicker continuously, leading to the trickery of Jacob and his mother to *steal* the inheritance with a bowl of lentil stew, roasted goat, and a goatskin disguise. Although Jacob garners the blessing, he flees for years with intense fear and anxiety, fearful for his very life related to the potential consequences of his deception.

How many times do we see the topic of fear addressed in the life of our Savior? From the announcement of the angels to the shepherds of Bethlehem to Easter Evening following the Resurrection in the Upper Room, we see the assurance from God in Christ, "Fear not! Shalom."

"On the evening of that first day of the week, when the disciples were together, with the doors locked for fear of the Jewish leaders, Jesus came and stood among them and said, 'Peace be with you!'... Again Jesus said, 'Peace be with you!'" (John 20: 19, 21)

So how do we commonly see the word *fear* used in God's Word? Most frequently, the Bible states, "We are to fear the Lord." This can be deeply troubling to some people in our culture. Our monotheistic (Judaic-Christian-Muslim) religions remind us that there are many things that we are to fear: Satan and other demons, crime, terrible and devastating natural disasters, contemporary domestic or foreign terrorism, and man-made catastrophes due to nuclear weapons, to name just a few. Don't we have enough to fear? Remember, the common denominator in fear is death (separation from God). But as a loving and caring Heavenly Father, why would the Lord tell us to fear God?

Fear in the Scriptures

The fear introduced to us in the Scriptures is a multilayered type of fear. It is a fear of being afraid of God's wrath due to our disobedience coupled with reverence and awe of our Creator and the family guidelines meant for our good.

Mora, a specific Hebrew term, was used in the Old Testament when referring to fear toward a divine or exalted being, which pointed to God. Interestingly, *mora* carried a meaning of terror. Also, however, in the Old Testament the Hebrew verbal adjective *yare* (fearful, afraid) meant to have reverence or respect. Used as a noun, the Hebrew *yirah* usually meant to convey "a positive quality or good intentions of fear of God." (Exodus

20:20) It was revealed in response to God's presence and Word (Psalm 119:38 and Proverbs 2:5) and opened a person to receive God's wisdom and knowledge. (Proverbs 1:7; 9:10)

The fear of the Lord that comes after the *Fall* generally does not yield pleasant results. It is associated with physical pain and hardship but also spiritual pain and anxiety as a result of the separation of our very soul from its relationship with its Creator. We do not just have a soul; we are a soul and we are a body, unique among God's creation. It's the kind of fear we most often associate with being confronted or threatened by impending danger, real or perceived. We worry about danger and its linked consequences and everything else in our future that is unknown. Adam and Eve learn fear because of their disobedience of God. Today, as we too still live after the Fall, there is fear due to disobedience—a fear of the Lord's wrath. That fear is appropriate. Hebrews 10:26-27 reminds us: "If we deliberately keep on sinning after we have received the knowledge of the truth, no sacrifice for sins is left, but only a fearful expectation of judgment and of raging fire that will consume the enemies of God."

However, fear in the sense of reverence and awe *also* still is possible in God's creation. As Israel sins after receiving the Ten Commandments, God shows power, might, and displeasure, on the one hand, in the thunder and lightning of the mountain. (Exodus 20:20) But then King David reminds us in Psalm 34:11, 13-14, "Come, my children, listen to me; I will teach you the fear of the Lord ... Keep your tongue from evil and your lips from speaking lies. Turn from evil and do good; seek peace and pursue it." The dual meaning of fear is still evident here; worry for the results of disobedience, and reverence for God's authority!

How does the New Testament describe fear? In the original Greek of the New Testament, the noun *phobos* is used, meaning to cause flight. But further in the New Testament we see the verb *phobeo,* meaning a wholesome dread of displeasing God, joined with reverence. St. Luke identifies this as a positive, productive fear, describing it to the early Christian church in this way, "Then the church throughout Judea, Galilee and Samaria enjoyed a time of peace. It was strengthened; and encouraged by the Holy Spirit, it grew in numbers, living in the fear of the Lord." (Acts 9:31) Fear of the Lord, then, should and can have an extremely positive effect; it can turn us toward obedience to God's will. Our fear of God's displeasure and its consequences and our reverence for God's majesty and authority can and is meant to be positive. Sadly, we know, we cannot accomplish this consistently nor on our own. Our physical and spiritual *genetics* continuously pull us toward disobedience and the negative effects of fear in our lives.

Furthermore, in the Old Testament, the *antidote* for our fear is promised; in the New Testament, the *cure* is made a reality. Because of Christ's atonement, we can now live a dual human citizenship or condition— as saint and as sinner, rightfully fearful, yet rightfully at peace in Jesus. Therefore, in both Psalm 34:11 and Acts 9, we see the result of fear being healed, producing a heart at peace.

We continue in that dual meaning of fear of the Lord in the Church today. But because of Christ, we also hope and trust in God's love, and our hearts find peace and wellness in the healing of God's presence.

Anxiety in the Scriptures

As you recall earlier in this text describing the characteristics of anxiety, I pointed you to a historical outline for the use of the actual word *anxiety* as found in the appendix. To review, the word and concept of *anxiety* (again, I am using this as a spiritual component of fear) was seen in the early writings before the time of Christ, and the concept of anxiety was probably understood by St. Luke as a physician of that time. The term *anxiety* was not used during a long span of history from AD 400 to the 19th and 20th centuries, although, as earlier noted, descriptions of *anxiety disorders* using other names were discussed in some medical texts in the 1600s and 1700s.

So we don't see the term *anxiety* in the original King James Version of the Bible because I believe that was not a term in general use during the 17th century, but translations that were written in more recent times do include that exact word. The King James Version was penned between 1604 and 1611. It used the Masoretic Text for the Old Testament and the Textus Receptus for the New Testament supplemented by some readings from the Vulgate. (Jerome's translation published in AD 382.) The word *anxiety* was not generally being used in medical texts or common conversation during the Middle Ages, from the fifth to the 15th century, nor in the Renaissance, the 14th to the 17th century.

However, in multiple writings of the early church fathers (prior to AD 400), we see prominent examples describing a spiritual worry or anguish of the heart or soul of mankind, particularly with the rumination of an impending future event, consequence, or situation.

Here are just a few examples of this soul disorder or soul distress (I believe a description of the word *anxiety* that we use today) from the *Confessions* written by St. Augustine of Hippo, consisting of 13 autobiographical books written in Latin between AD 397 and AD 400.[6]

> "Thou has made us for thyself, O Lord, and our heart is restless until it finds its rest in Thee."

> "I was in misery, and misery is the state of every soul overcome by friendship with mortal things and lacerated when they are lost. Then the soul becomes aware of the misery which is its actual condition even before it loses them."

> "I recall how miserable I was, and how one day you brought me to a realization of my miserable state...My heart was panting with anxiety and seething with feverish, corruptive thoughts... Goaded by greed, I was dragging my load of unhappiness along and feeling it all the heavier for being dragged."

"The soul is 'torn apart in a painful condition as long as it prefers the eternal because of its truth but does not discard the temporal because of familiarity.'"

"O Lord my God, tell me what you are to me. Say to my soul, I am your salvation. Say it so that I can hear it. My heart is listening, Lord; open the ears of my heart and say to my soul, I am your salvation. Let me run toward this voice and seize hold of you. Do not hide your face from me; let me die so I may see it, for not to see it would be death to me indeed."

There are a few other later church writers using the word *anxiety*, but they are living after the King James translation:

St. John the Baptist de La Salle (d. 1719): "Do not have anxiety about the future. Leave everything in God's hands for he will take care of you."

St. Gerard Majella (d. 1755): "Who except God can give you peace? Has the world ever been able to satisfy the heart?"

By the time the New International Version (NIV) translation (1973, 1978, 1984, 2011) and the English Standard Version (ESV) translation (1971) are on the scene, medical and psychological writings utilize the term *anxiety* commonly, (including the now widely recognized and approved DSM series) applying it to many well-defined mental disorders. Therefore I believe that is why we see the term *anxiety* occurring within the translations of the Scriptures in more recent years.

Let me share some examples from the NIV translation of the Scriptures of the use of the word *anxiety:*

"When anxiety was great within me, your consolation brought me joy." (Psalm 94:19)

"An anxious heart weighs a man down, but a kind word cheers him up." (Proverbs 12:25)

"So then, banish anxiety from your heart and cast off troubles of your body, for youth and vigor are meaningless." (Ecclesiastes 11:10)

"Therefore I am all the more eager to send him, so that when you see him again you may be glad and I may have less anxiety." (Philippians 2:28)

"Cast all your anxiety on him for he cares for you." (1 Peter 5:6-7)

The New Testament texts point to God's love in Christ, which is intricately reconnecting us to God's family through the grace of the Gospel, dispelling our anxiety of loss and separation. God's love in Christ reestablishes our relationship with our Creator.

We continue to fear God; we have disobeyed God's law and we are certainly guilty. Yet we do not have to be paralyzed eternally by our fear because we know and trust that God loves us and that we are God's through the forgiveness brought to us in Christ. This indeed is the life of the Christian. We know and accept that we deserve God's wrath, but by God's grace, through faith, we trust in God's mercy and love because God has forgiven us in Christ. Jesus comes from heaven, walks, suffers, and dies in our place on the cross, and then rises again. Jesus destroys the power of sin. Jesus destroys the power of death. Jesus reunites us to God's family and God's love. And in overcoming death and reconciling us with the Father, Christ offers us healing from fear and anxiety, and he removes our guilt and shame.

Is that not what we are invited to in the power of Christ through the preaching of the Gospel by our pastors when we are faced with a terror in our lives? When a new spot, a new lump, an alteration in our family dynamics, an uncertainty in our employment, or a challenge to our self-worth or vulnerability arises (all of which are components of loss and death), aren't we invited to respond with hope and trust and faith in God's love? It can be a real struggle to do so in the midst of suffering. But we are in continuous need of this Gospel message touching our hearts, minds, and bodies. It is our daily need. Especially in times of fear and uncertainty, in addition to our medical and psychological care, we need to hear God's Word through preaching, pastoral care, and the sharing of the Gospel. If anxiety indeed encompasses a spiritual component of illness, added to the healing of our physical being, we need our soul healed to be truly clean and truly whole. Spiritual care then is absolutely essential to healing, wellness, and peace.

Guilt in the Scriptures

The word *guilt* appears in the NIV translation of the Bible 109 times, and of those it appears only once in the New Testament in John 9:41. *Guilt* is used 119 times in the ESV version of Scriptures, seven times in the New Testament. It is interesting that guilt is predominantly a topic in the Old Testament, prior to the saving, substitutionary work of Christ (promised in the Old Testament, but fulfilled to us in the New) in his death for our disobedience and guilt.

Shame in the Scriptures

The word *shame* appears 122 times in the NIV, 13 of which are in the New Testament. In the ESV version, *shame* appears 141 times with 19 times in the New Testament.

Shame (the result of our disobedience or behavioral inadequacy) is dishonor, being put to the lowest place, the most despicable being, and unworthy of relationships. But the New Testament ESV version of Romans 10:11 places our lot as sinful human beings in the perfect light of Christ's love, "Everyone who believes in him will not be put to shame." Hebrews 12:2 says we are "looking to Jesus, the founder and perfector of our faith, who for the joy that was set before him, endured the cross, despising the shame, and is seated at the right hand of the throne of God." In Christ, our worthiness of relationship with God is restored, our shame destroyed.

I mentioned earlier, as we discussed care of those shamed, the concept of *shame resilience.* We Christians have a different understanding of the restoration of *shame resilience.* We know that this is received only by Christ's sacrifice in our place. In a moment, we will look at the liturgy of corporate worship, especially Confession and Absolution (and this applies to private confession and absolution as well) based on the Holy Scriptures as one way the Lord provides us with *shame resilience* as God builds our faith in the gifts of Word and Sacraments. Our worth is renewed; our membership in God's family is restored and assured in Christ. Our faith communities and fellowship with other members in the body of Christ become *safe places* to deal with shame.

However, dealing with shame in our congregations, denominations, and ecclesiastical structures can also present challenges as we recognize in a discussion of the anxiety, shame, and bitterness that might occur in the setting of congregational and denominational conflict. See Chapter Ten for a further discussion of these powerful emotions in the setting of church conflict.

Bitterness, Anger, and Malice in the Scriptures

Shame, when utilized by Satan in an individual's life, or especially as the devil may successfully use it to establish a foothold in congregational or denominational conflict, leads to a *shame-linked chain reaction* of its own. St. Paul describes this *linked chain reaction* in Ephesians 4:30-31. "And do not grieve the Holy Spirit of God, with whom you were sealed for the day of redemption. Get rid of all bitterness, rage and anger, brawling and slander, along with every form of malice." (NIV)[7]

Bitterness, particularly in professional church workers like pastors or teachers, as in all of us, is often displayed by cynicism when they feel they have been shamed or humiliated by fellow clergy, members of their congregation, associated faculty, students, parents, or ecclesiastical supervisors. That cynicism is defined by skepticism, suspicion, and distrust. Often, particularly in men, that bitterness and distrust become the foundation of rage and anger in the congregational or denominational setting, or for any of us in our workplace or home. The anger referred to here is not the *righteous anger* displayed by Christ as he drives the money exchangers out of the Father's house. This anger, rather, has at its root a negative, destructive, emotional discharge. The energy of that emotional upheaval of anger can get released in fighting via physical altercation or verbal abuse, name-calling, and slander, all in an effort to even the battlefield. The resulting malice (the intention or desire to do evil, get revenge, inflict suffering, animus) intends to harm another.

In female professional church workers, and again in any of us, bitterness can lead to anger and "getting back" at those who are provoking the bitterness, feelings of inadequacy, or shame, by internalizing negative self-talk. But this often occurs in the setting of the females' *mothering-sensitivity* where they may feel hurt, for example, by people who say, "So you're a teacher and look how your own children behave in public!" Alternately, the bitterness might be evoked comparing their skills, management abilities, or relational strengths as females to their male counterparts.

The Scriptures are filled with examples of bitterness, not just bitter-tasting food, but bitter lives (46 times in the NIV alone, both Old and New Testament). Here are just of few of God's people expressing such *bitterness*:

"Esau...burst out with a loud and *bitter* cry." (Genesis 27:34) This derived from his shame, humiliation, and embarrassment of being manipulated by his brother, Jacob.

The Israelites' lives were filled with "anger, *bitter* with hard labor," from their harsh treatment at the hands of the Egyptians. (Exodus 1:14)

From the mouth of Naomi we hear, "It is more *bitter* for me than for you [Ruth] for the Lord's hand has turned against me!" (Ruth 1:13) She feels alone and abandoned by the loss of her husband and sons.

"Don't call me Naomi," she told her. "Call me Mara, because the Almighty has made my life *bitter*." (Ruth 1:20) Mara is derived from the Hebrew word for *bitter*. This, from the great, great, great...great-grandmother of our Savior. Naomi, and Ruth for that matter, could have turned that bitterness into further anger and malice, thereby giving the devil a foothold. But through the mercy of an almighty God, she returned to her people in Judah, and their lives (and ours) were blessed by the revelation of God in the birth of their descendant, Jesus, in that very town of Bethlehem.

"See to it that no one falls short of the grace of God and that no *bitter* root grows up to cause trouble and defile many." (Hebrews 12:15)

In Ephesians 4, St. Paul suggests for us a far preferable emotional and relational life, that born of the saving work of the Savior. Rather than lives filled with shame, bitterness, and malice, St. Paul calls the Ephesians and us to "Be completely humble and gentle; be patient, bearing with one another in love." (Ephesians 4:2) Rather than wrangling, "Make every effort to keep the unity of the Spirit through the bond of peace." (Ephesians 4:3) Ephesians 4:7 says that "to each of us grace has been given as Christ apportioned it."

How, then, might we move from the bitterness, humiliation, and malice of shame to peaceful coexistence, harmony, and unity of spirit with our brothers and sisters in Christ? God's Word, the holy Sacraments of our faith, and the gift of absolution and confession—whether private or corporate—provide a beautiful format for the healing of bitterness.

Corporate confession and absolution based in God's Word and found in Christian liturgy of the Church provides a setting for this healing process. The liturgy of your denomination might be similar to ours in the Lutheran Church—Missouri Synod. I'll reference ours since this is where I faith-walk, and italicize my comments.

"Most merciful God, we confess by nature that we are sinful and unclean [*the very definition of guilt* and *shame*]. We have sinned against you by thought, word, and deed, by what we have done and by what we have left undone. We have not loved you with our whole heart and have not loved our neighbors as ourselves. We justly deserve your present and eternal punishment" [*and this is the essence of our guilt*].

[*Here we are at a crossroads. We can, by our sinful nature, guilt, and shame proceed, (as St. Paul reminds the Ephesians 4:30-31), to bitterness and wrath and anger, brawling, and slander, along with every form of malice. That would provide the perfect foothold for Satan to build a base of operations to separate us from God.*

But there is the Christ; there is his substitutionary death on the cross to repair our relationship with the Father, to remove our sin, guilt, and shame. Here, through the forgiveness offered by Christ, we have a new pathway; we are a new Creation. Therefore we have the opportunity to continue our prayer and our plea:]

"For the sake of your Son, Jesus Christ, have mercy on us. Forgive us, renew us, and lead us, so that we may delight in your will and walk in your ways to the glory of your holy name. Amen."

[*Next we hear the pastor/confessor announce this life-saving news to us:*]

"Almighty God in his mercy has given his only Son to die for you and for his sake forgives you of all your sins."

We are, through Christ, indeed healed!

CHAPTER 6

FEAR AND ANXIETY FROM A FAITH PERSPECTIVE

Thomas sits nervously in the waiting room of my office, displaying so much anxiety that my receptionist grabs my arm as I pass her desk and exclaims, "You'd better work that fellow in early. I don't think he's going to make it to his 3:30 P.M. appointment."

"Send him in," I sigh, looking at the stack of charts on the counter.

It is fortunate that we work Thomas in earlier than scheduled. Thomas is the youth minister at one of the community churches in our town. He is a hardworking and conscientious young pastor, spending hours doing private counseling to youth, coaching several sports at the local middle school, and organizing and leading retreats, fundraisers, and weekend outings for the congregation's bustling youth ministries. He has been married less than a year, and his wife is a teacher in the elementary school in the neighborhood; she is very conscientious in her own right.

Thomas faces perhaps the greatest dread of anyone working with or counseling youth.

One of the 13-year-old boys in the congregation just committed suicide. Pastor Thomas had spent substantial time with this lad and his family dealing with a bullying situation at school. Thomas had connected the boy with appropriate and credentialed counseling, prayed for and with the boy and his parents, and devoted many occasions to special interventions at retreats and church camp settings. Thomas thought the boy was coping better. Nonetheless the boy took his own life.

Now Thomas is convinced that he has failed as a pastor. His grief and anxiety are overwhelming; he is unkempt, fingernails bitten and demolished, eyes reddened from remorse, and the very image of Edvard Munch's painting, *Der Screi der Natur*, or *The Scream*.

Thomas looks me square in the eye and says with substantial conviction, "I am not only fearful for this boy's soul, I'm afraid for my own soul. I mean it; I'm a failure. I couldn't save his life. I thought I was bringing him back to balance with his family and his classmates, and I thought I had been helping him through all his worries and shame, building his faith, and helping him to see God's love despite what others were saying to him. I failed him! Where did I do wrong?"

Although I spent the next hour listening and preparing a plan to deal with the physical and emotional intensities ravaging this young pastor's being, I knew that he needed help way beyond my expertise. Thomas, as well as the boy's family, needed the care of a pastor, bringing to them the comfort and restoration of God's Son in the Word and the edifying presence of the Holy Spirit to be first and foremost in their lives. Thomas himself, and the parents, also needed Christian counseling to begin the process of working through the apparent guilt, and perhaps shame that this situation always seems to awaken, even in the most faithful of lives.

> *"Who shall separate us from the love of Christ?...*
> *Neither death nor life...nor anything else in all creation*
> *will be able to separate us from the love of God that*
> *is in Christ Jesus our Lord." (Romans 8:38-39)*

Our Christian faith tells us that, totally undeserved and only by God's grace, God gives us Christ Jesus to heal our fear and anxiety, guilt, and shame.

When Christians use the word *grace*, I think they mean the undeserved *love* and *forgiveness* from God brought to us through Jesus Christ's death in our place on the cross. Christ's sacrifice, that love and forgiveness, heals our fear and anxiety and overcomes our guilt and shame.

From the perspective of a physician who is a Christian, I am using three anchor points of faith to discuss fear with the lens of faith because, as a disciple of Christ, I (we Christians) know the source of healing power:

1. In the faith-building work of the Holy Scriptures, the Sacraments, and the power of the Holy Spirit, the healing power for our fears flows from the fountain of Christ's work and presence. Just as that healing energy flows from Christ (think of the woman with years of hemorrhaging in the Gospels of Matthew 9:18-26, Mark 5:21-34, and Luke 8:40-56), we Christians bear the responsibility of sharing that good news with those who suffer the ravages of fear and its cause, sin. I believe the Scriptures are the inspired and inerrant Word from God to creation. From the first book in Genesis to the last words of Revelation, the Bible points to the healing work of God's Son, Jesus.

2. Evil is a reality of God's creation gone awry, brought into creation through the self-desire of Satan, of Adam and Eve, and the daily self-desire of you and me. We place ourselves above the will of our Creator and destroy our loving relationship with God. With this evil in constant supply, why does God allow the pain of separation from our Creator (fear, as we have earlier defined it) to bring suffering to God's children? We believe God allows suffering, certainly in many instances, to "refine us by fire," knowing that this reduces guilt in the

midst of affliction and emboldens our faith. (Isaiah 48:10; 1 Peter 1:7)

3. God has, indeed, set in place from the beginning a glorious plan to restore our relationship to God. Because we have and continue to be disobedient by our very nature, the only restoration with God comes to us through our faith (as a fully undeserved gift—grace) in the obedient and substitutionary death of the Son, Jesus. That healing faith works and grows in us through the hearing of God's Word, through the reception of the Sacraments, our Baptism and the Lord's Supper, and the daily maturing of our faith through the power of the Holy Spirit.

These anchors provide a foundation for those who believe in Christ as their Savior. Does God heal non-Christians, those who don't confess Jesus as their Redeemer? Of course. God offers healing to all of creation and does so according to God's will, purpose, and glory. (See the story of the Syrophoenician woman's daughter in Matthew 15:21-28.) That God offers physical healing to all does not diminish our faith. But our firm belief as God's children is that God stands with open arms and freely offers us this whole, gracious healing of body and soul. Sometimes God offers this immediately, often through a process of healing over time, and for all of faith, ultimately in Christ's victory over death.

Now, what about fear itself from a faith perspective? As noted above, fear originates from the *Fall* of humanity, placing our desires above God's will for us, resulting in a broken relationship with our Creator. But there is also a *spiritual component of fear* that extends beyond the immediate physiologic reaction to danger. Animals respond with fear, many with the identical biochemical and neuromuscular reactions and secretions similar to humans. But the linked chain of fear, which we have identified earlier as *anxiety,* requires that the human creature is also a *soul* or *spirit*. Anxiety is a *spiritually encompassing, soul-distressing* aspect of fear.

What do I mean by *soul* or *spirit?* Most definitions of soul would include both the incorporeal (immaterial), and immortal (eternal, beyond time limits) essence of a living being. In the descendants of Father Abraham (certainly Jews, Christians, and Muslims) it is our faith that only human beings have been given immortal souls. Hinduism and Jainism consider all biological organisms and even inanimate objects to have souls. As a Christian, however, I trust the Scriptural words, that "God formed the man from the dust of the ground and breathed into his nostrils the breath of life, and the man became a living being [soul]." (Genesis 2:7) Man is a unique creation—not an angel, not a cherub, but a body-soul being.

When God's body-soul creatures, Adam and Eve, make their self-focused, self-desiring, and disobedient choice to seek equality with God in the knowledge of good and evil, they immediately usher in disorder, disease, and fear into the order and wellness of a healthy creation. (Genesis 3:10) As they invite in a physical creation gone awry, through supplanting God's will with their will, they also invite into creation a *spiritual* disorder to fear—and I am again calling that *anxiety.* Perhaps the most relationally destructive aspect of fear and anxiety that enters God's creation through the first couple's disobedience is the entrance of *shame.* (Genesis 3:7, Isaiah 29:16, Romans 9:33, Romans 10:11) Shame means, as a reminder, one is not only personally flawed but unworthy of relational connection.

Satan uses shame to try to separate us from the love of God in Christ. From the Scriptures we learn of this fallen heavenly being, Satan, perhaps being a cast-out angel. He is also known as Lucifer or the devil. Satan, we see from Isaiah 14:12, 1 Chronicles 21:1, and Job 1 and 2 as well as the prophetic writings of Ezekiel and Revelation may have been an angel who, along with other heavenly bodies, let the desire to be equal to the Creator cast them into disobedience and sin. Even the names, Satan (the *slanderer* in Greek) and *diablo* (false accuser) provide insight into the devil's use of shame to try to pull us from God.

Satan uses two great lies to try to destroy our relationship to God. First, he says that we can fully obey God's law by our own hard work and effort—which is, of course, impossible due to our *fallen physical and spiritual genetics*. Second, Satan tells us that we can undo the restorative work of Christ spoken to us in the Gospel if we sin hard enough. In other words, we can be so "defiled" (shameful) that there's no way Jesus could possibly cover those flaws and love us. These are both lies!

Let us be quite clear about Satan. Satan was the first to sin through prideful desires, preceding the choices of Adam and Eve. Satan does try to influence our soul by using strategies like shame. However, we sin, not because of Satan and Satan's cronies. We disobey God out of our own desires. God does not set us up to sin.

"When tempted, no one should say, 'God is tempting me.' For God cannot be tempted by evil, nor does he tempt anyone; but each one is tempted when, by his own desire, he is dragged away and enticed. Then, after desire has conceived, it gives birth to sin; and sin, when it is full-grown, gives birth to death." (James 1:13-15)

Adam and Eve were guilty of desiring the same knowledge of good and evil that God possessed, and they made a choice to defy God's clear and simple guideline for them. Don't eat that one fruit from the tree of the knowledge of good and evil, or you will die! Adam and Eve did suffer *death* and God's wrath and curse because they placed their desires above God's will and desire for them. (Genesis 3) We sinned in Adam through our desires (Hebrews 7:9-10), and we continue to sin. (Romans 5:12) Adam and Eve were guilty; they should be ashamed of their behavior; and so also are we guilty, and we should be ashamed. We don't need more *Satan* to convict us. We need a last Adam. (1 Corinthians 15:45) This is why Christ came, to remove the guilt and remove the sting (shame and finality) of death.

Adam and Eve are also the first family relationship of the human race, and this first family chooses not to trust in the complete goodness, authority, and love of their Creator; that defines their family-relationship to God. Before their disobedience they enjoy a healthy relationship and *their significant value* in their relationship with their Creator. When they disobey God, they lose the closeness of being in that family. In other words, Adam and Eve destroy the proper and healthy perspective of their relationship and worth to God as well as to each other, and for that they suffer spiritual *shame*. They cannot comfortably meet their Creator through the cool of the evening in an atmosphere of peace and trust. They are ashamed to even stand vulnerably before each other, a shame only God can uncover.

Rather, they begin to experience fear, anxiety, guilt, and shame. The basic source of these emotions is the death and separation (removal from the Garden and their relationship with God) that God promises them for their disobedience. (Genesis 3:2) Death and separation become the real consequences of a fallen creation. (1 Corinthians 15:26)

Here are just a few of the future-oriented components of separation and death, encompassing physical and spiritual consequences from sin of which to be fearful: "To the woman he said, I will greatly increase your pains in childbearing; with pain you will give birth to children. Your desire will be for your husband, and he will rule over you." (Genesis 3:16) Adam doesn't escape either: "Cursed is the ground because of you; through painful toil you will eat of it all the days of your life. I will produce thorns and thistles for you and you will eat the plants of the field. By the sweat of your brow you will eat your food until you return to the ground, since from it you were taken; for dust you are and to dust you will return." (Genesis 3:17-19)

God kicks them out of their relationship with their Creator. God bans them from the Garden. (Genesis 3:23-24) Physically removed from God's loving family relationship, they now experience the reality of spiritual death and spiritual separation. They are banished from Paradise, taking on pain, struggles, disease, sorrow, separation, and death—and all the fear, anxiety, guilt, and shame that accompany these terrors.

Furthermore, Adam and Eve's disobedience sets in motion for all humankind that sense of impending danger extending now to many objects and circumstances in creation: future harm and uncertainty, things seen and unseen, things real or imagined, all the constituent parts of anxiety—biological, emotional, and spiritual. It is exactly that diffused, future-focused fright and worry of the mind and heart that we have earlier defined as *anxiety*! Adam and Eve gain for us the immediate fear of God's wrath, plus the future anxiety of God's displeasure and punishment. Additionally, they, as we, suffer the persistent guilt and shame that rises in disobedience; it is an unworthiness of being in relationship with their Creator. God wasn't kidding!

Therefore their eyes are open to the potential nature of many things that are real or perceived as being dangerous, including their own relationship with each other. This causes them to shelter from God and shelter from each other by a shameful and guilty *hiding* beneath a leaf. They're on their own; therefore they had better be fearful and anxious! And on top of that, there is that *death* consequence.

"The wages of sin is death," writes St. Paul. (Romans 6:23)

Death is the common denominator of all the fear, anxiety, guilt, and shame that consumes us on our earthly walk. Death *is* permanent physical and spiritual separation from our Creator. We are flawed before birth due to the sin of our first parents, Adam and Eve. We know we too are guilty of causing this flaw. We understand we too are not worthy of a relationship with our Creator. If that was all we had in our future—fear, anxiety, guilt, shame, separation, and death—what a horribly anxious and hopeless lot we would be. Yes, death remains for our flesh the *enemy*.

But our faith assures us that Christ has conquered death!

For those who believe that the promised Seed became flesh in Christ (Genesis 3:15, John 3:8, Romans 16-20, Galatians 4:4), the One who died in our place to fulfill the Law and restore our relationship to God, that physical and spiritual death for us of faith is *not* eternal. Even before God removes them from the Garden, God extends the promise of restoration of God's family in the Seed, Jesus.

Additionally, God also extends the promise to reestablish God's family in Abraham, Isaac, Jacob, and their descendants, the children of Israel. Abraham shows a willingness to trust in God and obey God's commands. In contrast to Adam and Eve's newfound fear and anxiety, we are reminded of Abraham's willingness (desire) to trust in God and obey God's commands. In Genesis 22:11-12, the angel of the Lord comes to Abraham as he is tested with Isaac and says, "Do not lay your hand on the boy...Do not do anything to him. Now I know that you *fear* God."

I would believe Abraham could have been very anxious when there was nothing to sacrifice except Isaac. God had expressed a good will, and Abraham wanted to fulfill God's will and supplant his own desires. If Abraham's son, Isaac, was the only option for sacrifice, Abraham was willing to submit to God's desires. Abraham feared God's wrath, but also reverently respected and trusted in God's will to provide. Here we once again see a dual component to Abraham's fear as a member of God's family—both fear and awe/trust.

And God brings healing, again to God's family through the provision of the Lamb, and the promise of the Seed. The Seed, the New Adam, the Last Adam, the Christ, was completely obedient to his Father; he was without sin. The full healing, the ultimate healing of our fear and anxiety (our biological, emotional, and spiritual fears), the removal of our guilt, and the dismissal of our shame is ours by grace through faith in Christ's death and resurrection, his submission of self to the good and gracious will of his Father.

Because of the New Adam, Christ, our fear is conquered and shame devoured in God's perfect love. 1 John 4:18 tells us, "There is no fear in love, but perfect love casts out fear. For fear has to do with punishment, and whoever fears has not been perfected in love." When we are brought into God's family in our Baptism because of Christ, we enter God's family of perfect love. (1 John 4:13-21) And it is God's family that lives without shame. (Romans 10:11)

In our Christian life and death, Jesus is the antidote, the solution, the resolution, the answer, the healing of fear, anxiety, guilt, and shame.

This does not mean that Christians are exempt from suffering, as I mentioned earlier—and for emphasis, let me say it again. In faith, we turn again to the New Testament: "And we know that in all things God works for the good of those who love him, who have been called according to his purpose." (Romans 8:28) Yes, our faith convinces us that God allows suffering to *refine us in the fire.* Our faith also assures us that all things, including pain, worry, fear, physical illness, mental illness, and even death have a purpose in God's plan. God worked out a plan for restoration of creation (and that includes you and me) from the beginning. From the first Adam to the Last Adam, God set in motion a glorious plan to gather people to God's family, through the promise of a Redeemer who would conquer pain and suffering, sin, and death. Jesus was glorified through his death and resurrection. (John 7:39, 11:4, 12:16; 1 Peter 1:21; Acts 3:13) Both the Father and the Son were glorified in the Resurrection. (John 11:4, 13:31-22) You know, sometimes we just can't see that from our time-confined perspective. It is our natural state to continue to hope for, and often expect, healing *now.*

Nevertheless, our faith prayer is that God, through the Holy Spirit and the gifts of grace, comforts and carries us through our times of sorrow and suffering. God's promise and will for us is *ultimate healing,* despite the physical illnesses of heart disease, cancer, and neurological collapse, and despite the mental and emotional illnesses of anxiety disorders and depression.

All in God's restored family look forward to a time when we join God in eternity, a place with no fear and no evil. (Revelations 21:27)

I love Christian hymnody in that it beautifully and succinctly encapsulates a theological truth. Let me share the second verse of that great Redeemer hymn by Johann Ludwig Conrad Allendorf from the mid-1700s, "Jesus Ist Kommen, Grund Ewiger Freude," based on Isaiah 12, Luke 1:68-79, and 1 John 1:1-2:

> *Jesus has come! Now see bonds rent asunder! Fetters of*
> *death now dissolve, disappear. See him burst through*
> *with a voice as of thunder! He sets us free from our guilt*
> *and our fear. Lifts us from shame to the place of his honor,*
> *Jesus has come! Hear the roll of God's thunder!* [8]

Spiritual Gifts to Face Fear

As I lead Grace Place Wellness Retreats for clergy, parochial teachers, and other church professionals over the last 18 years, I often ask, "How many of you offer health or healing ministry within your congregation?" Out of a group of 20, two or three will raise their hands. I'm quite sure they think I'm referring to "parish nursing" or "Stephen Ministries" or the like. I then ask them, "How many of you offer the Word of God and the Sacraments within your congregation?" And of course, everyone responds affirmatively and the light bulb goes on!

No matter what causes us to be anxious, we as God's family have grace-gifts to build and bolster our faith, to help restore energy to move from being anxious, shameful, and frightened, to being hopeful and trusting of Jesus, our Redeemer. We readily have God's gift of healing fear and anxiety. Here are marvelous spiritual grace-gifts we have been given to face our fears as faithful Christians.

God's Word

Our time in God's Word, including reading and hearing the Word as well as our ongoing study and catechesis (religious instruction) of God's Word, form the cornerstone of healing anxiety and reestablishing a healthy fear of the Lord. Meditation and continual learning of and reflection on the Commandments assist us, beginning with the First Commandment, "You shall have no other gods before me." We remember that we should "fear, love, and trust in God before all things." (Exodus 20:3) The act of meditating and praying on the Word is not a talisman that sheds our fear, anxiety, guilt, and shame. The power is in the holy Word of God acting directly upon our body, mind, and spirit.

The entire purpose of the Scriptures is to point to Jesus and his substitutionary work to restore our relationship with our Creator.

We use the Lord's Prayer and the confessional creeds (common statements of truth and our beliefs) of our church to reflect on and keep God's Word in front of us regularly. Keeping God first leads us to live out our life after our Baptism and affirmation of faith from a heart that fears, loves, and trusts the Lord alone. We often refer to Christ as the "New Adam" or "Last Adam" created without sin and living without ever sinning. We can't keep God's Word in our hearts and minds without the New Adam (Christ) because we would, by our sinful, Old Adam nature, prefer to have other gods, especially ourselves. We Christians believe that when we hear God's holy Word, the Holy Spirit brings us God's love and forgiveness by grace through faith in Christ; Jesus brings love and reconciliation.

Biblically based preaching of the Word through the pastor's sermon or homily is another powerful conduit for bringing calm to our fearful illnesses. Commonly, the pastor begins the sermon message by asking the Holy Spirit to be in the meditation of our hearts and minds as God's Word is shared with us. Hopefully, and most appropriately, the pastor's message is anchored in God's Word in the Bible. Although it is helpful to work other writings of literature into the message, the power of the pastor's reflections comes from sharing God's words and will for us from the Scriptures.

I would also suggest that praying God's Word in devotional time, meditatively, or in corporate worship is a helpful and appropriate way to fear and love the Lord.

As one resource, I would invite you to look more closely into meditatively praying God's Word in the appendix under "Word-Saturated Meditative Prayer." Meditatively praying God's Word has a long tradition in many communities of Christian faithful.

Baptism

The only way we can return to our family relationship with God is to be drowned, to have our fear, anxiety, guilt, and shame consumed by Christ's substitutionary death. This is received by us as a free gift in the water, Word, and anointing of the Holy Spirit in our Baptism.

Baptism imparts to us the faith to receive our new relational identity as a part of God's family. Our worth now becomes one of being a child of God, with Christ as our brother as well as our Savior. We recognize God as Love, as Protector, as Healer, as Head of our Family. (1 John 4:17-18, 1 John 4:8, Romans 8:15) Death has no power over us since Christ has overcome death. (1 Corinthians 15:55-57) Believing this truth when fear, anxiety, guilt, and shame begin within us (in those times that we feel we are not living up to the expectations of others, especially God's, or those expectations we set upon ourselves), we can remember the life restored to us by grace in our Baptism. Our Baptism lets us know the outcome of our human journey; it lets us know the beginning and ending to our book as a Christian. If we understand and truly believe how it all comes out in the end of this earthly journey, we are given the saving resource, through Christ, to overcome fear.

Holy Communion

Like Baptism, God provides people with another outward sign and means of receiving grace and forgiveness: the Lord's Supper or Holy Communion. I love the way St. Ignatius describes Holy Communion as "medicine of immortality, the remedy against our having to die." In the Large Catechism, Martin Luther calls the Lord's Supper, "a pure, wholesome, soothing medicine which aids and quickens us in both soul and body. For where the soul is healed, the body has benefited also." [9]

As we approach the Lord's Table to receive Christ's body and blood, we connect our death and resurrection to Christ's, begun and received in our Baptism in Jesus as we reflect on the words of institution.

Jesus gives us this sacred meal for those of us weakened or unsure of our faith in his saving and substitutionary work so that those of us who are anxious, sleepless, and exhausted by the trials of our daily walk can find a place of peace and rest at God's table.

Christ's meal blackens out our bad record before God. The Lord's Supper works and strengthens our faith that Christ's perfect obedience even to death is substituted for our fear, anxiety, guilt, and shame. In Psalm 130:3-4 we read, "If you, O Lord, kept a record of sins, O Lord, who could stand? But with you there is forgiveness." That is what Holy Communion provides for us.

Confession and Absolution

In confession and absolution, whether corporately or privately, we have a way of daily renewing our Baptismal covenant. We have an opportunity to die to sin and rise to life in Christ. Confession and absolution call us to daily repentance and forgiveness. Confession means we are saying the same thing as or assenting to what God says. In confession we admit and declare that we are indeed guilty! We speak this out openly and freely before God.

As with the Lord's Supper, confession and absolution provides a pathway to practically carry out our daily Baptismal walk far beyond our mental remembrance of having been baptized. It is the Holy Spirit's continuance of the faith begun in the water, Word, and Spirit's anointing. It involves the Spirit's maturing and strengthening of our faith but rest assured, the Spirit is present from the moment of our rebirth in Christ.

In many faith communities, confession and absolution are confined for the most part to corporate worship and often preceding the celebration of Holy Communion, or the Lord's Supper, or the Eucharist. But the practice of private confession can have benefit, especially as it joins us to our abiding connection to the gracious love and forgiveness received in our Baptism, and our daily need to confess and repent our sins before God (dying to sin, and rising to new life in Christ).

As a human being, one created out of the dust and DNA of a sinful universe after the *Fall*, and being bound by the chains of sin and enslaved to my fear and anxiety, how beautiful it is to hear the voice of God saying, "I love you; you are forgiven because of my Son. You are mine." I long to hear that with sound waves on my eardrums and feel that reverberating into my heart. Those precious words of God bring comfort, hope, courage, and energy to my living and serving, and wellness and peace to a troubled heart.

CHAPTER 7

FACING THE FEAR OF WHAT MIGHT BE

David, a 58-year-old bright and highly educated husband and father of three teenage children, comes in for an unscheduled visit to my office. Upon entering the exam room, I detect terror in David's facial expression, body posture, and quivering voice. "I think there's something really wrong with me, Doc," he says, "I've seen blood in my stool again." "So this is not the first time?" I ask. "No, I've noticed it off and on for over a year," he answers with an obvious sense of guilt and remorse. He blurts out ashamedly: "I know I should have come in when I first saw it but—" here it comes— "...I was so fearful of what might be..."

> "He will cover you with his feathers, and under his wings
> you will find refuge; his faithfulness will be your shield
> and rampart. You will not fear the terror of night, nor the
> arrow that flies by day, nor the pestilence that stalks in
> the darkness, nor the plague that destroys at midday. A
> thousand may fall at your side, ten thousand at your right
> hand, but it will not come near you." (Psalm 91:4-7)

There is another aspect of fear that I have seen so often as a physician and that is the *fear of what might be*. It is the fright caused by a new physical ailment. It is the anxiety over the future consequences of a new illness. The apprehension, the sense of danger, is so debilitating that the fear itself affects the way we make choices about how and when to find out what is going on inside of us. Frequently that anxiety is also accompanied by guilt. *What have I done to myself to bring about this catastrophe? What physical and spiritual crimes have I committed against God, my own body, or creation itself, to bring about this disease?* And that anxiety is accompanied by shame. *I am embarrassed to death to admit to anyone that I am vulnerable, flawed, or even susceptible to illness. This will surely separate me from family, my relationships, and life itself.*

Too often our initial reaction to something new or different from what is normal for us is *denial*—what I would call a natural and self-protective but unhealthy response. We use tremendous emotional and spiritual energy convincing ourselves that illness happens to others but not to us. Sadly this emotionally cognitive, spiritually soothing strategy just doesn't work for long. Once we have abandoned this reframing of our perception and, of course, the *new finding* is still there, we often become paralyzed; we freeze; we avoid or delay discovering the origin of the danger, real or perceived, because we are fearful or feel ashamed.

Coping Strategies

Coping strategies we use to deal with fear and anxiety are often learned in our family of origin, although on occasion we come up with these strategies all by ourselves. Some of us use coping strategies we learn from the myriad of psychological self-help shows in the media. Generally, however, we cope in the same way as we observed in the lives of our parents.

What are some of the coping strategies we commonly use to face these fears produced by *changes in our wellbeing*? Sometimes we convince ourselves that if we don't clarify the real source of our fear, then our fear must have no basis in reality. This represents further denial—that we have nothing to fear. Or our response might be to hide from the fear by diverting our thoughts with busy activities. We may also try to replace our apprehension with more pleasant thoughts on other less stressful subjects. We may turn to emotional reasoning, where we allow our fear and apprehension to influence our perception of reality. For example, "I am fearful and therefore there must be something to be afraid of." In reality there may not be a real danger. Our fear and anxiety become a self-fulfilling prophecy.

Further, our fear, anxiety, guilt, or shame over the discovery of a threat often cause us to strike out at others by blaming or criticizing them for our distress. Alternatively, we may hide from our closest loved ones like our spouse or our children. We disconnect; we disengage from our support system.

These coping strategies can temporarily calm our emotional sense of alarm and the physical symptoms that often accompany fear of discovery. These strategies are utilized often by us to face threats, but they falsely bring a pause to our fearful emotions. We bury our heads and hearts in the proverbial sand. We try to assuage our guilt and shame by creating a hardened shell around ourselves, or making ourselves seem invincible to others. Unfortunately we still don't know what to do when the abnormal sign or symptom persists or returns, which it usually does.

Finally, perhaps on the rarest of occasions, we somehow muster up the courage to face our fear head on, approach it by defining it and dealing with it. Frankly, because it moves us more quickly to clarifying action, that response to a fearful threat is far healthier. But that is a vulnerable, courageous, and mature response; we have to admit we are flawed, and we require the empowering motivation to seek help.

Let's return to our friend and patient David with whom we began this chapter. David became paralyzed by his fear and then anxious of discovering colon cancer. This fear was not totally unfounded in that he was well aware that colon cancer was in his family history. His father died at age 60 of that very disease. Despite his mother's urging to have colonoscopies starting in his mid-forties, he had been too anxious about discovering whether he had a fate similar to his dad's. He felt guilty and then felt miserably ashamed of his self-care choices. He had used up all the denial he could muster, and so he became emotionally paralyzed, leading to inaction.

His subsequent work-up showed that he did *not* have cancer, but he *did* have polyps of the nature that if left alone, most probably would have become malignant. The polyps were the root cause of bleeding. I removed the polyps through a colonoscopy. David was fortunate, but so many folks delay evaluation because of fear, anxiety, guilt, and shame and suffer the same unfortunate end as David's dad.

I saw David in a follow-up visit about a month after his colonoscopy. Part of our conversation drifted into his personal life and especially how he felt so much more at peace. I asked him if that was just because he had "dodged the cancer bullet" by seeking care for his fears and anxieties. He told me something most reassuring.

David did pursue the cause of bleeding with me, as his physician, out of anxiety. However, he did so right after he sought the counsel of his pastor. Did David's fear and anxiety drive him to seek answers from God's Word? I think it did. But I believe David turned to God's Word because the Holy Spirit was already at work in David's heart, working his faith established in his Baptism. I think David found the courage and energy to seek care because of God's Word and promise to always be with him. And so it should be for each of us.

CHAPTER 8

FACING THE FEAR OF CANCER

Jenny is a nurse supervisor at our neighborhood hospital. I know her family well, and this highly accomplished young woman is about to be married to a terrific medical colleague of mine. Jenny appears a bit embarrassed at her office visit, even for a medical person, and simply says, "I have a soreness right in the pit of my stomach, boring deep into my back. It comes on about 20 minutes after eating, almost every time. I just feel so full all the time. It's weird, right?"

"Are you losing weight?" I ask. "Are you trying to get into a smaller wedding dress size?" I feebly attempt to joke.

"Actually, yes," she says. "I'm losing weight, and, no, I'm not trying! It's just coming off." And now a real furrow enters her brow. "I've actually noticed this off and on over the past six to eight months, but I've been so busy with wedding plans and stuff," as her voice begins to quiver.

This conversation introduces a very sad and increasingly painful two years, the last two years of Jenny's life. Subsequent to our office visit and weeks of extensive testing, Jenny is found to have pancreatic cancer, buried deep in the tail of the pancreas and hidden behind her stomach. "She's too young for that type of stuff," I grudgingly remark to myself.

She did get married, despite the known diagnosis, and she and her husband fought courageously, seeking care at the major cancer centers in our country before Jenny lost her earthly battle with cancer.

The shining beacon of grace in Jenny's story is that she was a strong woman of faith, as is her husband and her family. I believe Jenny invited others to faith in the way she faced and fought cancer. Hers was a battle laden with times of hope, and fear, and anxiety. Although there may have been bitterness, anger, or blame, I never heard it from Jenny. With each step in this journey, Jenny knew there was fear of what might be next. Most of those fears were experienced as reality, as is often the case for those of us facing these terminal diseases like cancer, heart disease, or neurological and muscular dysfunction. Jenny, however, put her faith in the only one who could relieve her distress ultimately and remove her pain as God called her to the home her Savior had been preparing for her forever.

> *"Praise be to the God and Father of our Lord Jesus*
> *Christ, the Father of compassion and the God of all*
> *comfort, who comforts us in all our troubles, so that we*
> *can comfort those in any trouble with the comfort we*
> *ourselves receive from God." (2 Corinthians 1:3-4)*

Although there is the fear of what might be, there is, of course, unfortunately quite often the fear of what truly *is*. The fear is about something very *real*, and that frightening *reality* needs to be faced.

I want to talk with you about the fear of cancer, since I know that fear firsthand. You see, I am a cancer survivor, and I thank the good Lord for granting me healing. Let me tell you my story.

I have suffered all my life with a congenital kidney defect, having been born with defectively formed kidneys. I did not know that medical fact until I became ill. I freely admit that now every time I go to the doctor I am fearful he will find a deterioration in my kidney function.

Within the first month of finally beginning my medical practice in the 1970s, I developed kidney symptoms suggestive of stones. This in itself was frightful and paralyzed my spirit for a time. Following lots of prayer with my wife and a visit with my pastor, I sought an evaluation through a urologist within my medical group.

To this day, I vividly remember the scene. My urologist came down to the X-ray department, and took me into a quiet room. "Well, we have some good news and some bad news. First, we can't see your left kidney at all. We do see your right kidney, which is huge; it compensated for the little guy on the left. Oh, and the kidney we see appears to have a lump on it. The kidney drainage system is all messed up. And of course you have stones!" he said.

"Could there possibly be any good news?" I wondered anxiously.

"The good news," stated the doctor, "is that your blood tests measuring your kidney function are all normal. I don't know how, but they are indeed normal. And, well, there's that lump on the big kidney."

I experienced some relief, but that was quickly followed with renewed terror. By the way, this was many years before the advent of sonically busting up kidney stones, such a common treatment today. It was also before newer radiologic diagnostic tests like CAT scans or MRIs were readily available. "So," explained the doc, "we're going to have to slice into your flank, cut out the stones, reconstruct the drainage system and..." he paused "biopsy that lump. I'm not kidding you; you know as well as I do that we are concerned about the lump being cancerous. You'll be in the hospital about three weeks and out of work for at least six more. Furthermore, if that lump is cancerous, well, you could possibly lose that kidney. And we don't see enough of a backup kidney on the left."

Great.

Wow. I had been in medical practice for only about a month and had been married for only a couple of years. Talk about the "fear of what might be"!

In the following weeks, I came before the Lord in prayer frequently. I didn't know where else to turn. I can say without equivocation that without the presence of Christ and the Holy Spirit ministering to me and comforting me and my wife, bringing a sense of sanity and hope through Scripture-based prayer and the Lord's Supper, I truly doubt I could have well endured that trial.

My window in my third-floor room at Lutheran Hospital in St. Louis looked directly across the street at Holy Cross Lutheran Church. My dear pastor visited me and gave me and my family the Lord's Supper the night before surgery. We shared God's promises and prayed even to take this cup of fear and illness away. But we also prayed for God's will for healing to be done. I did, indeed, feel the prayers of many prayer warriors around the country. A beautiful picture of Christ in Gethsemane was at the foot of my bed. I'm sure you know the painting. I fell asleep and slept deeply only to be awakened by the nurse at 4:00 A.M. the day of surgery.

God's good will was done that day. The stones were removed; the lump was a benign cyst; and the drainage system was repaired. The kidney and my life were restored and spared. God be praised.

In many facets this story repeated itself in my life some 40 years later, but this time with the discovery that I had prostate cancer. Additionally, post radical prostate surgery, I lost what remained of the defective left kidney. However, I see how God's steady hand of healing through the surgery on the right kidney allowed me to lose the left kidney and still preserve good overall function. I am faithful to my yearly appointments despite having momentary times of continued concern and worry, and I don't have prolonged anxiety. God has now granted me the energy to clarify my fear and the faith to trust God's power of healing, whether that is immediately, gradually, or ultimately.

I have learned that I have to turn all of these fears over to the Lord. I have understood the critical importance of faithfully exchanging the immediate reaction of fear for trusting, honoring, and respecting the Lord's good will for me. Am I 100% faithful to addressing fear in this manner? No, but the Holy Spirit knows I am a work in progress and continues to faithfully care for and encourage me daily.

I also understand that there will be a time when the Lord knows that the only way to heal my ills is to ultimately heal me by bringing me to Christ's side in eternity. I am journeying in Jesus' presence with a peace that passes all understanding, and that comes by God's grace through faith in Jesus' death and resurrection for me and the world. When that time comes, and it will, I hope you will be praying with me. Be clear, it's not faith that heals. It is Jesus and his perfect sacrifice for my flawed and unhealthy being that heals.

For those of you who are facing the very real fear of cancer, I will assure you that the "coping" paralysis that arises from your fear of discovering the truth is nothing compared to the eventual suffering that might come from far-advanced disease if your symptoms are left unaddressed. Trust the Lord; fear the Lord; sit at the feet of the Lord to receive comfort and healing. God's promise is to always be with you, refine you, heal you. As the Lord says, "So do not fear, for I am with you; do not be dismayed, for I am your God. I will strengthen you and help you; I will uphold you with my righteous right hand." (Isaiah 41:10) That's *God's* promise.

If you receive a diagnosis of cancer, it is common and normal to feel anxious and panicked. As you consider calling on the Lord in prayer, consider several additional aspects of your cancer diagnosis that you can meditate on in prayer.

- How advanced is your cancer?

- What treatment options are available to you?

- What other type of support do you have around you? Are there personal family members, pastors, a church family, professional counselors, or nutritional and physical therapists to call on? It is critically important to share with your doctors and therapists what anxieties and concerns you might have in dealing with cancer. Merely verbalizing your fear may help you feel empowered. Your medical team can explain the progress of your illness and therapy in more depth and provide counseling or teach you relaxation techniques. Your spiritual resources can bring the Word of God to you, remind you of your Baptism, encourage and share prayer, and bring you the Lord's Supper.

- Do you have financial considerations as a result of your illness and the need for further planning for your future or the future of your loved ones?

I think there are also existential anxieties that come to play in dealing with illnesses like cancer. *What is my purpose in life in light of this potentially lethal disease? What does life mean to me, for me?* These are subjects worth raising with your physicians, your pastor, and your support team in your faith community.

Additionally, not just the cancer itself but also the accompanying fear and anxiety may produce symptoms like sleeplessness, lack of appetite, irritability, lack of concentration, and the desire to isolate yourself from friends and family. You may slip into a significant sense of depression. Several additional physical sensations are common with anxiety and depression and may originate from just the fear itself rather than the tumor, chemotherapy, or radiation therapy. Palpitations of the heart, sweating or body shakes, shortness of breath due to hyperventilation, fatigue, nausea, diarrhea, or even constipation due to pain medications, tense muscles, abdominal pain, ringing in the ears, and reddening or pallor in the face can all occur just from your anxiety.

These many and varied symptoms may occur because anxiety causes your body to release adrenaline in preparation for the fight-or-flight response. Our body and our emotions are preparing us to face danger, especially in circumstances like cancer.

Your medical care team might suggest counseling or even medication to help reduce anxiety, and both can be helpful. However, once again, I believe you can turn to meditation and prayer based in God's Word, and this discipline can be a most powerful and effective therapy. Once again, please see the appendix for a discussion of Word-saturated meditative prayer.

One major fear with illnesses like cancer is worry about pain. Cancer patients worry about whether they will experience pain or whether the pain might be more than they can bear. It is not uncommon for patients with cancer to not experience significant pain. Others with cancer clearly suffer substantially. God has blessed us with many wonderful pain and anti-nausea medications. Additionally, there are many wonderful non-medicinal pain control therapies available, and your healthcare team will help you find those treatments, perhaps through a pain clinic. I deeply believe the more you understand about your pain and what you can do about it, the less fear and anxiety you will experience.

Anxiety arises when discussing treatment plans with our doctors. Fortunately we live in a time where huge advances in therapy, especially for cancer, are occurring daily.

Here are a few certainties of cancer care and treatment in the 21st century:

- Radiological, chemotherapies, and immune treatments, including stem-cell and bone marrow transplants, are far easier to tolerate than before and substantially more successful.

- The side effects of these therapies are often easier to control than in the past, especially regarding the gastrointestinal tract and nausea.

- Gene mapping and the use of individual and customized therapies based on your genetic markers hold tremendous hope for less destructive, less invasive, and more curative treatment for many cancers in the near future.

I strongly recommend the importance of being maximally informed about the possibilities for your therapy when you visit your doctor. Here are a few suggestions to help you stay informed:

- Make a list of questions gathered from consultation with your physicians, family, and even Internet exploration. Ask them all.

- Don't feel foolish if you don't understand what the doctor says. Ask your questions again.

- Have close family or friends with you to take notes and ask questions.

- Ask the doctors for time to think over your options for care and treatment.

- Seek the best care you can find, and don't be afraid to ask for a second opinion.

- Get online or ask your care providers for counseling organizations and support groups for your particular illness. These resources can be invaluable to you and your family.

All of these recommendations will be helpful in diminishing the anxiety you have about cancer. When anxiety is reduced, your road to recovery and healing can be much enhanced.

CHAPTER 9

FACING THE FEAR OF DEATH

We recall our friend, nurse Jenny, from Chapter Eight. Jenny faced not only the fear of cancer, but the reality of death due to her disease. As members of the human race, we know that unless Christ comes soon, and very soon, we each will face death due to our human physical and spiritual genetics. Unless our death is sudden and unexpected due to disease or trauma, we will all likely face a period of fear and anxiety about what's to come.

> *"The Lord is my shepherd; I shall not want. He maketh me to*
> *lie down in green pastures: he leadeth me beside the still waters.*
> *He restoreth my soul: he leadeth me in the paths of righteousness*
> *for his name's sake. Yea, though I walk through the valley of*
> *the shadow of death, I will fear no evil: for thou art with me;*
> *thy rod and thy staff they comfort me." (Psalm 23:1-4, KJV)*

One common denominator of our medical fears is the fear of death. Many folks with any terminal malady, cancer or otherwise, experience an overwhelming fear of dying from their disease. Furthermore, many people in general have an acute fear that death may occur from a sudden heart attack, stroke, or a traumatic injury like a car accident or life-threatening infection. Finally, many people, sick or not, have a fear of the potential pain related to death and symptoms often associated with dying—like choking or paralysis, or the loss of recognition of their loved ones at the end of life.

Allow me to resume my story, as I have experienced that real fear of death too.

I previously revealed to you that I am a cancer survivor. In 2012, I was diagnosed with prostatic cancer of an aggressive variety, and underwent a radical surgical resection of the cancer, and the removal of lymph nodes. I assure you there was plenty of fear and anxiety surrounding that operation.

The surgery was ultimately very successful and I have been cancer free for five years. Praise Jesus for his goodness. But the story of healing was not smooth and not without setbacks. In my case, the healing came gradually over time and with a strong dose of tempest.

I mentioned earlier that I had a congenitally deformed drainage system from my kidneys to the bladder, causing the development of kidney stones 40 years ago. Six weeks after prostate cancer surgery, I suddenly became overwhelmingly sick, with a high fever, chills, and nausea. This led to a prompt return to the emergency room at, incidentally, the hospital where I was a very active internist and gastroenterologist for many years.

After a series of blood tests, X-rays, and an abdominal CAT scan in the emergency room, I was diagnosed as having a ruptured diverticulum or pocket originating in the colon. I was admitted, seen by many of my fellow physicians, and was started on high dose of intravenous antibiotics, along with a complete bowel rest (no food) for nearly a week.

After a week I was no better. I still was having severe fever and chills, although I was not experiencing abdominal pain. Actually, I never had pain with any of this.

Sometimes God uses strange and circuitous pathways to heal people. Early on a Sunday morning after the first week of hospitalization, a new young surgeon was making rounds on behalf of his surgical team, and came in to let me know I was probably going to have to go to surgery in the next 24 hours.

But this young man *stopped* to do a thorough reexamination and to look back over all the tests. Good thing! God thing! He returned about an hour later saying that the diagnosis of a ruptured diverticulum made no sense to him—and it didn't to me either, but I wasn't exactly thinking clearly. He immediately ordered a repeat abdominal CAT scan and returned with a broad smile to say, "There's no evidence of diverticulosis. You have a massive pocket of pus in your defective, tiny, left kidney. It isn't draining and that's causing the bacteria in your blood!"

This made much more sense, I thought, and I was relieved. "So, we need to get you down to interventional radiology, and get that kidney drained with a tube into your flank, and change the antibiotics," the doctor said. "Hallelujah," I responded. This was Sunday at noon.

However, I waited and chilled continuously all Sunday afternoon and night, all Monday morning and afternoon, waiting to be taken to get the drainage procedure in radiology. "They're incredibly backed up with patients," was the repeated message. By this time, I was shaking with chills so vigorously that they had to pour the medications into my IV just to try and control the tremors. About 4:30 P.M. Monday, they came to get me with a gurney. I was shaking so uncontrollably that for the first time in my life I truly felt as if I was going to die. In fact, I remember waiting another 45 minutes in the preoperative room, spending time thinking through my worries and concerns for my wife, children, and ministry that would have to carry on without me. The reality was that without rapid intervention I was likely going to die.

My agony, emotionally and physically, was pretty overwhelming. I knew that the only place I could turn was to prayer in Christ's name. I was praying while they set me up in the radiology suite and for another 30 minutes as

I waited for the interventional radiologist to arrive. Now here came the really cool part. I suddenly heard an Arabic-accented voice somewhere in the room say, "Why is this fellow still lying here?" Barely raising my head, I recognized the voice of my good friend, a Palestinian-born physician and one of the best interventional radiologists in St. Louis. This physician's hometown was Bethlehem, Palestine. He came as an adviser and translator with me on one of my many trips to the West Bank where I worked with a Lutheran church, school, and parish nurse program right in the little town of Bethlehem. He is Muslim and he even invited me to experience the closing of Ramadan with his family in Amman, Jordan, on one trip. He just happened to be passing by that radiology room on the way out of the hospital, as he had been working in another facility all day.

"Please help me," I know I cried.

Within seconds, he expertly inserted a drainage tube into my side. Within moments my temperature came down, and I began the process of healing. My God and Lord did not leave me. God brought healing through my friend and fellow physician, one with whom I had walked in Jesus' footsteps in the Holy Land.

Now I do understand that people with terminal cancer or other life-threatening illness may have their prayers answered in *different* ways. I said it before but I will say it again, because it is such an important point: God heals.

Sometimes God heals in miracles (and I have seen that as a physician on occasion). Just as we learn in the Scriptures, every once in a while—and perhaps more often than we can imagine—God removes disease immediately without scientific or medical explanation. I have seen that very infrequently, but I believe I have had a few cases like that in my medical practice. Sadly, the response in most medical situations of "spontaneous healing" is that the physicians will say, "Well, the X-rays just weren't read correctly," or, "That tumor seemed to melt away; I guess it was really responsive to that combination of chemotherapy and radiation." Perhaps, just perhaps in these situations, God chose to touch people for healing like he did the woman who had hemorrhaged for 12 years (Mark 5:25-34, Matthew 9:20-22, Luke 8:43-48) or the 10 lepers (Luke 17:11-19) with spontaneous miracles.

However, most of the time, God heals in a process and over time. In Mark 8:24-25, we are told of a blind man who comes to Jesus for healing. Jesus touches the man blind from birth, and after this first touch, the man says he can see. But his vision is very blurry; he sees men walking around like trees. Only when Jesus touches him a second time does his vision become clear. Why would Jesus heal *gradually?* Jesus always heals with a purpose and his will in mind. Looking at other complementary passages in Mark, might it be that Jesus is teaching his disciples (and the blind man) that each of us has rather cloudy spiritual vision or spiritual nearsightedness as well? (Mark 8:18) It occasionally takes us time to come to a realization of Jesus' power of healing our bodies, along with a healing of our souls or whole healing. Whole healing, complete healing, only comes through Jesus.

We also can reflect on the raising of Lazarus, the brother of Jesus' long-time family friends, Mary and Martha of Bethany. (John 11) The sisters plead for Jesus to come to heal their brother. Yet Jesus stays away for a purpose—to bring glory to God before he returns to Judea (where, incidentally, the people had just tried to stone the Lord). When Jesus arrives at Bethany, Lazarus has already been in the grave for nearly four days. However, in the building of the faith of the sisters, his disciples, and anyone who would listen and believe, Jesus calls Lazarus back to life. And the Scriptures tell us in John 11:45, "Therefore many of the Jews who had come to visit Mary, and had seen what Jesus did, believed in him." Sometimes, I am convinced, it takes a bit more time for us to recognize the healing of our hearts and minds along with the power of healing God has placed into our bodies.

Finally, there are times God heals ultimately, through removing the pain and suffering by bringing us to Jesus' side. As a physician, the fact is, I know that God is the only one who can really relieve the suffering from many illnesses. Sometimes, the only way that happens is to bring those suffering so deeply into the arms of Jesus in eternity. "'I am the resurrection and the life. The one who believes in me will live, even though they die; and whoever lives by believing in me will never die. Do you believe this?' 'Yes, Lord,' she replied, 'I believe that you are the Messiah, the Son of God, who is come into the world.'" (John 11:25-27) Again, in John 14:3, "And if I go and prepare a place for you, I will come back and take you to be with me that you also may be where I am"—a place of eternal wellness, peace, and joy.

My experience is that most people with terminal illnesses and most Christians that I have been with near death are not anxious. They develop a peace that surpasses all rational and human explanation and understanding, especially after they have heard and prayed in the Word, perhaps received the Lord's Supper from their faithful pastor, said their goodbyes to family, and prepared to fall asleep in Jesus. That is a most beautiful and holy death. May God grant that to us all.

Such a death is peaceful.

But I don't mean in any way to minimize or whitewash death.

Let's look more closely of what we know and believe as Christians about dealing with death and the grief that accompanies it. I will admit that I cannot talk about death from the non-Christian perspective, other than to say that without my faith in Christ, I believe I would find no solace or comfort believing that there was merely void after death, nor that somehow "death is the old person's friend." What I know about death is that it is a horrible reality for all of us unless Christ returns very soon. Death is the enemy, the curse of Adam and Eve due to their disobedience, and our curse because of placing our desires above those of our Maker.

God's desire for us is life, life forever, and even *abundant* life. (John 10:10)

Scripturally, we as baptized Christians are dead as we speak. "But if Christ is in you, your body is dead because of sin, yet your spirit is alive because of righteousness." (Romans 8:10) Even we Christians must die. The Bible teaches us that at death our mortal bodies lie in the grave and our souls are immediately joined with Christ. We rest until body and soul are reunited with Christ. I've spoken to pastors from many Christian denominations about this "in between time, the time between the moment of death and the last coming of Christ." I've often heard questions people express like, "Is Grandma up in heaven peering down on me and everything I do?" Many theologians suggest that upon death, the construct of time for the deceased person ceases to exist. If we die in Christ, our next "conscious" moment is the resurrection of all the saints on the Last Day, with healed bodies united with their souls to glorify God forever. It all happens in "the twinkling of an eye," as the Bible says. (1 Corinthians 12:51-52)

I don't know all the details, nor do you; but I do know this by faith. For those in Christ, death is a victory. And in the process of that death, in the dying, Christ Jesus walks with us in the valley of the shadow of death. So we will have no fear.

What happens if we do not believe in the saving death of Christ on the cross when we die? Well, we are told in Revelation 20:14 that there is a second death in which unbelievers' souls are immediately joined with Satan in the eternal punishment of hell. That saddens me and all those walking in faith in Christ, unimaginably. I am incredibly sorry to share that bit of news with you if somehow you have never heard it before, or if you prefer to reject this notion, or rationalize our destiny as humans at life's end, or even scoff at the idea of a *hell*. But if that makes you anxious, or fearful, or even raises a glimmer of questioning, please don't be paralyzed. I urge you to seek some clarity and understanding in God's Word offered through a pastor, or church, or even someone who you know to be a follower of Christ. Give them the opportunity to open God's Word up to you. And if you cannot find anyone to speak with, contact me.[10]

So in the meantime, how are we, as Christians, to deal with dying and death? We must keep our eyes on Jesus. Christ's promises in God's Word become more powerful and comforting. We recall Christ's magnificent words to us in John 14:2-4: "In my Father's house are many rooms; if it were not so, I would have told you. I am going there to prepare a place for you. And if I go and prepare a place for you, I will come back and take you to be with me that you also may be where I am. You know the way to the place where I am going." What great comfort these sweet sentences provide to us as we live, and as we die.

Just let me add one word about dying in these current times. I believe through the development of hospice programs (now readily available throughout the world) that we are coming to our senses as a culture, and perhaps returning to a more dignified process of dying, compared to the last 100 years. My comments do not apply to assisted suicide, for which I can find no Biblical support.

As we look to the care committed to the last six months of life in this country, we see that incredible financial and medical resources are used up in the later stages of the dying process. It consumes a major portion of the community healthcare and family fiscal resources in many circumstances. A great deal of this frantic activity is really because of fear, fear within the person who is dying or, more commonly, fear within the dying person's family.

I believe, medically and socially, we may have matured, especially when we consider the use of hospice or similar end-of-life support services. Hospice used to be thought of as merely providing pain relief when facing terminal cancer. But now we have broadened our parameters to utilize hospice care for anyone facing end-of-life illness, including congestive heart failure, chronic obstructive lung disease, end stage kidney and liver disorders, neuromuscular illnesses like ALS or MS, muscular dystrophy, as well as many others.

There are specific treatment guidelines for a multitude of illnesses, but basically most people qualify for hospice (according to the National Hospice and Palliative Care Organization) if they are entitled to Part A Medicare and certified as being terminally ill by a physician, and have a prognosis of six months or less to live if the disease runs it normal course. There are a few more requirements and these might range from circumstance to circumstance, age to age, or insurance company to insurance company, but that is a broad general guideline. Your physician can provide you with many resources if you find yourself faced with end-of-life decisions and need for resources.

The purpose of hospice care is for the person to die in dignity and with comfort and, as much as possible, without anxiety.

I have experienced hospice care with my own parent, and I know many of you have as well. It is a marvelous complement to any family's end-of-life care, and to the Christian family and their faith community, as they deal with the care of their saints in their last days on earth.

CHAPTER 10

FACING THE FEAR OF CONGREGATIONAL AND DENOMINATIONAL CONFLICT

I probably don't have to share a specific story of conflict within your faith family. If yours is like mine, and I suspect it is, I'm sure you have some yarns of divisiveness and dysfunction that you can spin within close reach of your consciousness. However, I wonder how many of us are truly aware of individuals, whether clergy or laity, who have actually suffered substantial emotional and relational trauma as a result of these conflicts? Please pause for a moment to consider that question because it may even be you yourself. I assure you, this is a real source of strife for many, and a stumbling stone for faith and function, especially for those deeply embedded in church service. The accompanying fear and anxiety from conflicts in faith communities are often intense and need to be addressed.

> *"Just as a body, though one, has many parts, but all its many parts form one body, so it is with Christ. For we were all baptized by one Spirit so as to form one body—whether Jews or Gentiles, slave or free—and we were all given the one Spirit to drink. Even so the body is not made up of one part but of many*

(vs. 12-14)...But in fact God has placed the parts in the body, every one of them, just as he wanted them to be. If they were all one part, where would the body be? As it is, there are many parts, but one body (vs. 18-20)...On the contrary, those parts of the body that seem to be weaker are indispensable and the parts that we think are less honorable we treat with special honor (vs. 22-23)...But God has put the body together, giving greater honor to the parts that lacked it, so that there should be no division in the body, but that its parts should have equal concern for each other. If one part suffers, every part suffers with it; if one part is honored, every part rejoices with it. Now you are the body of Christ, and each one of you is a part of it (vs. 24-27)...And yet I will show you the most excellent way (v. 31). (1 Corinthians 12)

Organized groups, whether they are social, political, cultural, or religious, can, in their diversity, system-nature, and dysfunctional relationships, devastate the emotional and spiritual lives of some of their members. These organized groups are often bound together by a common set of "beliefs" or "goals, values, and mission statements." In fact, religious denominations and congregations, and even subsets within a denomination or congregation, may well have more homogenous characteristics than other societal groups. And yet, particularly within Christian congregations and denominations (the only faiths where I have experience of caring for their members), there is, indeed, diversity in the midst of the unity. Diversity itself is not evil. Diversity has been a part of God's good Creation and the foundation of Christ's Church from the beginning. However, when Satan and ME-orientation (inward direction to the group's energy, thinking, decision making, response to others with different views) establish a foothold amid diversity, then conflict may begin to dominate relational harmony.

Yet within all groups, despite tenets that would teach otherwise (see most of St. Paul's writings to the early church), there may be elements of *competition, comparison,* and *conflict.* Even though, most typically, there are very vocal factions who hold intense opinions and feelings (and occasionally express outbursts of hostility and freely verbalize their displeasure), the vast majority within a religious group is relatively *silent.* This less vocal middle majority may be sympathetic with parts of both sides of the more extreme points of view. In fact, this middle group might appear to some to be a bit less informed, or merely less passionate about the topics that seem to produce the intense feelings at the edges of the faith body. In fact, the middle majority can be very well informed and also may have the capacity to embrace nuanced positions. And sometimes the middle majority might merely exclaim, "why can't we all just get along?"

Religious denominations appear to be more likely than most to explode into passionate internal warfare, with extraordinarily devastating effects on members of leadership (such as parish pastors or bishops), educational influencers, or even individual members of their congregations. Both clergy and laity may find the very foundation and core of their emotional and spiritual stability threatened, resulting in a fear and anxiety-based "fight-or-flight" response to conflict in full display.

Sometimes that "fight-or-flight" response may be internalized within congregations or individuals with devastating personal injury, but on occasion it is externalized and in very public sight. Bitterness may abound. Sadly, slander, anger, and malice may not be far behind.

Each *group* in these disagreements is convinced that God is "on their side"—or, conversely, they are on God's side—and what's more, they utilize the words of Scripture and historical or contemporary confessional writings to back up their position. This can make for stunningly convincing apologists. However, as each side strives to demonstrate its *rightness,* Satan has an opportunity to gain a *foothold,* a *base of operations,* to encourage bitterness and slander by encouraging the sides to take things the other group expresses, even out of context, in order to support their own beliefs. Furthermore, Satan also encourages people to put second or third things first, urging us to forget or neglect what is truly of utmost importance.

I am concerned that these types of explosive conflicts are poorly handled by all faiths, whether Christian, Jewish, Muslim, or others, both at the denominational (national) and congregational (local) level. We know of the vitriolic behaviors among Christian and Jewish sects past and present and have dramatic examples in recent times among the Shia and Sunni populations of Islam. As a physician who is Christian, I have seen the devastating trauma repeatedly in patients I have doctored from multiple Christian denominations who have been caught in this emotional/spiritual grinder; psychiatry, counseling, and clergy colleagues report substantial incidents of the same nature. As a frequent visitor and worker in the Christian community in Bethlehem, Palestine, I have seen firsthand the violent infighting within the religious caretakers of the Church of the Nativity over such things as who is sweeping on which side of a demarcation line, or who is cleaning which stained glass window or religious icon.

Is there wisdom from the disciplines of medicine and psychology and, most importantly, from God's Word, to guide us as participants or as caretakers in these conflicts to foster repair, restoration, and reenergizing for living and service to these suffering individuals? Of course we Christians understand the real healing is in the heart and hands of our Lord and what God has done for us. Exodus 15:26 says, "For I am the Lord that heals you."

In all of these conflicted relationships, there appears to be two essential but complementary processes necessary to bring peace to the hearts of those struggling: *conflict resolution* over the issues that divide and *spiritual reconciliation* of personal and sin-based underpinnings before God and before those with whom we are in conflict.

Conflict Resolution

Perhaps these conflicts are "organizational-relational" disorders that require resolution more than "faith" disorders, but when one's faith and faith community are integral to the conflict, lives and work can be fundamentally disrupted.[11]

What do we understand from a medical, psychological, and spiritual perspective to care for *people* caught in these religious conflicts that produce so much anxiety, shame, bitterness, anger, and malice? Most counselors would suggest that in individuals in conflicts, the reality is that you can really only change the behavior of "your side" in any conflicted relationship. You can try mightily to impose your will on that of the opposition, which may gain a temporary and tenuous pause in the conflict. Most often you will merely harden the hearts of those you suppress, and heighten their bitterness, slander, anger, and malice to be displayed at a later time.

But can you change the behavior of those with opposing views, let alone those who have slightly different perspectives within your own *group*? As an individual, perhaps you possess the emotional maturity to handle your words and feelings regarding the topics causing confrontation and conflict in your congregation or denomination. However, it may be very disturbing to you to hear those who believe as you do but are communicating and handling the conflict poorly. How might you, as an individual in conflict, or as a caregiver to those in conflict, serve as a *leaven of reconciliation* in the name of Christ in the setting of diversity and disagreement?

The fact that we, by our sinful nature, choose sides, selecting often to be adversarial rather than allying, sets up conflict and even schism. This "survival of the fittest" mentality, so predominant as we look at our secular society, places our personal agendas ahead of the health and wellbeing of the whole society in which we live. Noted psychologist and clergyman Rev. Dr. David Ludwig often refers to this as placing ME ahead of WE. It is a turning inward of our hearts, spirits, and minds to concentrate on what is in our own best interest. Our focus is on ME or my like-minded group, rather than what's best for the greater good of all people—what David refers to as WE. It seems that today's evolutionary anthropologists believe that is how civilization advances.

However, great spiritual voices like St. Paul, (Romans 7:15, 18-19; 1 Corinthians 12; Ephesians 4), St. Augustine, and 16th-century reformist

Rev. Dr. Martin Luther in his Lectures on Romans, remind us that the inward focus of our being (*incurvatus in se*) is the very definition of humanity's captivity to the self-centeredness of sin.

How does the ME attitude lead to conflict in church organizational relationships? Most every Protestant denomination, the Roman Catholic faith, Judaism, and the Muslim sects, demonstrate divisions over doctrinal, structural, and control/leadership/political power topics. Each *side or group* utilizes deeply reasoned, felt, and inspired arguments to *prove* their doctrinal (core teachings, learnings, beliefs) conclusions to be *correct*, and even the very will of God, as proven by God's Word and as clarified by theological scholars and apologists. Each side declares to be faithful to these specific truths, understandings, and confessions *to the death.* Additionally, there is always the fear of the *slippery slope*—if we give in on one little point of contention or conflict, who knows where any of this might end?

I accept, very honestly and sincerely, that each *group* in these conflicts and disagreements, each *part of the body of Christ* for us as Christians, finds great emotional and spiritual stability and comfort in their beliefs; they want to honor and be obedient to God's Word. This is particularly true as they express their beliefs as a part of a *group of homogenous spirits* with similar doctrinal interpretations, missions, and goals. At face value, that might seem like a *WE-oriented,* or a unified, solidified posture. To the contrary, I would suggest to you that it may end up being used, when grasped by Satan, to produce a *ME-oriented* approach to diversity and conflict.

Why would I suggest that this could be a *ME-orientation* to disagreement? Well, the ME-orientation, of course, is the core of original sin, the turning inward described by St. Augustine and Martin Luther as referenced above. So what happens to those outside of ME? If you find yourself in a group with beliefs in conflict with another part of the faith body, it may be that your opinion, worth, legitimacy, and authority are at the least challenged and often rejected. Even beyond being rejected, you as an outsider may be aggressively attacked and slandered in an effort to *purify* your *errant* thinking or beliefs and in an attempt to change or even reform your side of the relationship crisis. I wonder if Satan is somewhere near at hand?

Some of these church battles may just arise from the prodding of the devil, and thus, original sin. This may be spiritual warfare in its most blatant form. Once Satan establishes a foothold within our individual bitterness of being disrespected, maligned, and our worth challenged, (Ephesians 4:26-27), our hearts and minds may become closed, hardened, nontransformable, and constricted to the healing process. Hardened and constricted hearts wallow in sin. Paul reminds us in verses 29-32 from Ephesians 4, "Do not let any unwholesome talk come out of your mouths, but only what is helpful for building others up according to their needs that it may benefit those who listen. And do not grieve the Holy Spirit of God, with whom you were sealed for the day of redemption. Get rid of all bitterness, rage and anger, brawling and slander, along with every form of malice. Be kind and compassionate to one another, forgiving each other, just as in Christ God forgave you."

As we look at Paul's writings in the early chapters of Romans, we see plenty of theological firepower aimed at those who would *add* or *subtract* from God's Word in the Scriptures, and rightly so. However, is it possible that our fellow Christians, whom we recognize all as saint and sinner just like *we* are, might still receive God's undeserved love and forgiveness, just as *we* will, because of Christ's substitutionary death on the cross for us *all*? I pray your response is, "Yes!"

But more commonly, at least within Christian denominational communities, the *conflicted groups* often prefer to label each other or even themselves as being more *conservative* or *confessional* interpreters of the Word versus more *liberal,* or *socially sensitive,* or *missional,* or *evangelical* followers of Jesus. It is easy to see the use of *group labeling* as derogatory and as a slanderous statement and malicious attack on not just the others' beliefs but also on their personage as a child of the same heavenly Father.

Those attacks become fundamentally and personally disruptive, destructive, and life-threatening, especially when one's faith is at stake. When we attack our brothers and sisters, even ones with a different expression of their beliefs or application of doctrinal confessions to daily life, are we *causing ones who believe to stumble* in their faith? (Mark 9:42)

Conflict is not new to the Christian Church, and the harm inflicted on brothers and sisters of same faith is hardly novel. Paul, Barnabas, and the *sides* in the debate over the Gentiles even among the Jewish Christians of Jerusalem were embroiled in sharp disputes. Yet in Acts 15:10-21, the Holy Spirit brings wisdom and reconciliation. "Now then, why do you try to test God by putting on the necks of Gentiles a yoke that neither we nor our ancestors have been able to bear? No! We believe it is through the grace of our Lord Jess that we are saved, *just as they are.*" (italics added)

Again, from Paul we recall, after the purity he urges in the earlier chapters in Romans, that he closes with these final thoughts in this pivotal book to the early church, "Let us therefore make every effort to do what leads to peace and to mutual edification...So whatever you believe about these things [*here Paul is speaking to the Jewish Christians of Rome regarding life-practices, eating, or drinking*] keep between yourself and God. Blessed is the one who does not condemn himself by what he approves." (Romans 14:19-23)

Then Paul goes on to conclude, "We who are strong [*and those strong might be, perhaps, those with spiritual maturity to act as peacemakers*] ought to bear with the failings of the weak and not please ourselves. Each of us should please our neighbors for their good, to build them up. For even Christ did not please himself but, as it is written: 'The insults of those who insult you have fallen on me....' May the God who gives endurance and encouragement give you the same attitude of mind toward each other that Christ Jesus had, so that with one mind and one voice you may glorify the God and Father of our Lord Jesus Christ. Accept one another, then, just as Christ accepted you, in order to bring praise to God." (Romans 15:1-7)

No matter which *group* of the theological debate team you cherish and associate with, is it possible *to disagree with and hate what you and your compatriots see as the offense, and yet love, and care for, and edify the offender?* Again, I pray your answer is "yes."

Fundamental Attribution Errors Due to Poor Listening Skills and Bias

Let's look at other causative features of the fear-anxiety-shame-bitterness linked chain leading to malice inflicted on fellow members that can result from diversity, disagreement, and conflict in religious communities.

A second underlying cause of conflict in individuals and in groups is what Dr. Ludwig labels as a "fundamental attribution error." In relationships, we *think* we are sure what the other person is saying and even inferring when, in fact, we might totally misunderstand the other's point, intention, context, and character. The same error applies to denominational groups and subgroups. A fundamental attribution error means that while I attribute my behavior to a certain situation or set of circumstances, I attribute your behavior to your character. In social psychology, this is also called *correspondence bias* or *attribution effect.*

Sometimes we don't understand our opponent's style. Or, because of our internal bias, we presume their character or their intentions, rather than consider what external factors might drive their communication or behavior. In contrast, we interpret our own behavior or our own communication style as the gold standard.

Here's an example of what I mean. I am driving down a city street and it begins to rain ferociously. While coming to a stop sign, the rear of my car fishtails and I slide out into the intersection, fortunately without causing an accident. A moment later, another driver approaches the intersection to my right. He slides as well into the intersection and ends up grazing my bumper. My response is that he is a careless, irresponsible driver. Whereas I was just as unfortunate to hit a slick spot on an oily street in an unanticipated rainstorm. Hmmm.

Another way to gain insight into these attribution errors, Ludwig notes, can be to better understand each other's communication styles. Some people, he suggests, are "painters" and others are "pointers." See the appendix to help you determine which you might be in any given communication interaction.

Painters communicate their thoughts and feelings by *painting* a picture filled with color, various levels of energy, small strokes, large strokes, throw-away comments, references to past and unresolved conflicts, or disagreements; this especially pertains to communication of deeply felt emotions. The first words out of their mouths may not be the point of their communication; in fact, they may not even realize the point of their talking until they have applied the many strokes of their *painting*. They process predominantly *externally* and *verbally*.

Pointers, on the other hand, communicate verbally but only after they have processed their thoughts *internally*, and often *silently*. The first comment from their mouths is the *point* of their communication. They strive to gather information, think internally and silently through the data, categorize it, organize it, and then communicate their conclusions. They can come across rather droll or dry, unless their communication mate finds ways to gently scroll down deeper into the pointer's emotions through focused, same-subject questions. Pointers' brains are a bit "computerlike." Their mate must listen closely, sometimes a challenge for painters, to what the pointer is saying; then the painter may find key words in their pointer's communication. By repeating those key words, exactly, the painter may help their pointer open deeper files within the pointer's emotional files. Once opened, the pointer can be every bit as verbally expressive and emotional as their painter partner.

Pointers, how can you help your painters communicate more effectively? First, Dr. Ludwig reminds pointers, "don't try to *tell* your painter what *they* are thinking or trying to say." Don't try to *solve* the emotional feelings the painter is trying to express. Don't try to calm them down by shortcutting their processing or expressiveness, even as you feel you are *helping* them resolve their distress. Saying, "Oh, I know exactly what you are trying to say or what you're feeling" will drive your painter bonkers! This aggravates the painter and, in essence, shuts them down. Rather, pause, speak gently and understandingly rather than patronizingly, and encourage them to *paint on*! This approach honors the painter's processing, gives the painter the time and space to get their thoughts on the canvas, and allows them the luxury of seeing the picture in all its fullness and vibrancy.

Are these communication styles fixed in any given person? No, they are relationship-specific; most of us float somewhere in the center of painting and pointing, depending on a given relational communication. Some of us point at work and paint at home. However, others use painting or pointing more consistently as their communication style.

If you think about it, you probably see this in your communications with loved ones at home, in work settings, within church councils or faculty meetings, and even in larger denominational settings.

Are these communication styles gender specific? No, although Dr. Ludwig feels, based on his longstanding experience, that about 75% of women are painters, and 75% of men tend to be pointers. However, that leaves 25% of males as painters, and 25% of women as pointers.

Consider, then, how these communication styles might affect conversation and understanding within your faith family. Perhaps, more pertinent to the church diversity topic at hand, how might communication styles lead to deep and divisive conflict within the family of the church, or even the band of clergy leadership as they attempt to shepherd their congregants, or each other? We may well have a *listening* weakness. It is difficult, even within the body of the faithful, to dwell in peace, let alone find resolution to secular and spiritual challenges, if we are not *listening* to each other, or especially if we are not listening to God's communication to us through the Word. When we *pause to* initiate our interpersonal conversations, particularly in our faith family in the setting of prayer on God's Word, cognizant of differences in individual communication styles, we may listen to each other better and understand each other more fully. Placing our conversations in the setting of praying God's Word, especially together, may also allow us to honor and respect our conflicted neighbors as fellow members of God's family. We give them their rights and worth as family of God members just as Christ has done for us, even though we may disagree with their given assessment of a particular challenge, social or organizational problem, or application of a part of the Scriptures.

I believe that when our Christian forefathers (for example, St. Augustine, Luther, or 20th-century German theologian Friedrich Bonhoeffer) urge us to *pray the Word,* they are suggesting that, as we enter prayer to God, we begin by conversing in God's words, praying the Holy Scriptures, praying the Psalter, praying in the language with which God speaks to us. In such *Word-saturated prayer,* through the power of the Holy Spirit, the listening of our very hearts is further opened to hear and understand God's will for us. Again, I will refer you to the appendix to learn more about this Word-saturated meditative prayer discipline.

This is one communication skill, learning to listen, that may help us avoid *fundamental attribution errors,* substantially reduce organizational anxiety, and bring a far healthier psychological and spiritual environment within our denominational or congregational system, in order to move onward in mission despite conflict.

I believe once we *truly listen* to our neighbor with whom we find ourselves in conflict, we may find that folks who are labeled as *confessional,* indeed, have a vigorous heart for Christ's Gospel *mission,* and those labeled as *missional* or *evangelical* hold intensely fast to the common *confessions* of our shared life in Christ, the One Body, and One Faith, One Baptism.

Sadly, those of us who care for professional religious workers and leaders frequently encounter those individuals who are under attack by others in their faith community. They may present for care with physical signs and symptoms of a stress-related nature such as heart, immune, metabolic, or neurologic ills. Most often, rather, they are emotionally overwhelmed by fear, anxiety, shame, humiliation, and bitterness. If not cared for properly in body, mind, and spirit, they can easily slip toward depression, anger, self-destructive behavior, or malice.

Finding the Core of Fears in Congregational and Denominational Conflict

So often, within congregational and denominational conflicts, there appears to be so much disharmony and anger flowing from the contentious parties, that it is hard to see, let alone imagine, a way toward unity, or a way toward joint constructive service.

Frequently, I would suggest the basis of that turmoil, and unfortunately, elements of malice toward the other in conflict, is not anger, but rather the core topic of this book: there is deep-seated fear.

Often at the foundation of that fear there is a stealthily buried, intensively felt *defining moment* or *precipitating event* that sets up the cascade of fear-related, automated, emotional sequences that have long been forgotten or buried beneath layers of relational rubble.

Those defining moments, also described by Dr. Ludwig, are most vivid when they occurred and when they can be recalled. They may be suppressed within our memory bank to buffer us from the pain they induce. However, they may show themselves repeatedly in both subtle and dramatic forms whenever similar circumstances or moods rise to the surface, or sometimes even when the status quo is merely threatened.

These defining moments often are partially or even completely *fear-based*. That fear may, again, be anchored in loss; e.g., we can't move to a new sanctuary and tear down the old one because my dad built the old church by hand. Or we can't change the Sunday school time to accommodate the new worship schedule because my mom was the head of Sunday school hour, and she worked tirelessly each week to have the lessons and activities prepared to go off like clockwork at 9:30 A.M. each Sunday. Or I grew up with the liturgy of the old hymnal; the new contemporary worship just is not worshipful enough; what would my sainted parents think? Or I remember a time when we were short of ushers and let a woman usher for Holy Communion Sunday, and in the blink of an eye there were women ushering at every service, and one is now running for head of the ushers' club. Before you know it, women are going to want to be pastors, bishops, or church body head executives!

Often, unless we can get to these defining moments or crystallizing events precipitating our fear, we can't resolve the conflicts dividing us. Most frequently, getting to those core fears, again, is not something we can achieve through self-diagnosis or self-treatment, especially when it might involve two sides within a conflict. It requires a wise and experienced counselor to help each side discover the core fear(s).

And until we unearth the source of those wounds and those hardened hearts, and until we bring those fundamental fears to the light of recognition and awareness, we can't begin the process of addressing understanding and healing. We can't comprehend what is necessary for us or our conflicted brothers and sisters in Christ to confess to each other, and seek and grant absolution and forgiveness.

As we will discuss in a moment, the beginning step in this confession and forgiveness process is for each person in the conflict to acknowledge and then confess their *own* sin and shortcomings before God, and receive God's forgiveness in Christ.

Sometimes we need facilitators; we may need peacemakers to guide us.

Who and Where Are the Peacemakers?

In addition to improving communication and listening skills and getting to root causes of fear, are there additional strategies for changing from an adversarial relationship to one of greater harmony or *allying* toward a common mission and goal? A complementary component to this question is who, within or outside of the organization, can initiate and facilitate peace?

Again, from Dr. Ludwig's counseling experience, one further strategy might arise from a better understanding of how we resolve conflict. Incidentally, the same principles I am about to discuss are equally applicable to personal conflict resolution within your own home. There are several pathways toward conflict resolution. The first may be to spend substantial time in *defining* the parameters and core of the conflict, or *naming* the conflict. This is a favorite strategy of individuals with a painter-style of communication. However, defining tends to cause the two sides in conflict to move *against* each other as each side stakes out their territory with vigor and more clearly defined correctness in the hopes of *intellectually or emotionally convincing* the other side of the *truth*. Honestly, it is a ME-focused attempt at reconciliation.

A second approach might be to *avoid* conflict and move away from each other. This is a pointer-style approach, which unfortunately tries to bury the conflict below the surface of the relationship, hoping to lessen anxiety and tension. Again, this is a ME-approach leading ME to feel better but not healing the division in thinking or emotion. Sigmund Freud discovered how truly unhealthy this approach is to resolving conflict in the human being.

A third strategy, again ME-focused, is for both sides in the conflict to merely move *toward* the conflict in the hopes of *keeping the peace* at all costs.

Unfortunately although a temporary emotional ease can be achieved, the core of the conflict is not dealt with, and the conflict will rear its ugly head once more later.

There is a fourth approach to resolving conflict. It's tough and takes a lot of commitment, work, and energy, but it probably offers the best chance for healing. That strategy involves making an *ally* of your enemy. It starts by first forming a *healthy relationship* with your opposition, fostering better understanding of each other's viewpoint by using healthy communication skills, acknowledging the other's deeply held beliefs, and then realizing your own potential fundamental attribution errors. As you are focused on listening, you may even forgive them for what you perceive is harm against you, which gives back to them their rights and worth within the relationship.

Finally, you now can expend maximum energy *moving together with your ally* to solve the conflict. This is a WE-approach to conflict resolution and it offers the best hope for sustainable peace, and emotional and spiritual healing. Of course, an essential step toward an allied relationship is confession and absolution, and we will address that shortly.

As wise theologians and writers like Frederick Buechner, or the more contemporary Max Lucado and David Ludwig remind us, "Conflict is inevitable; combat is optional." Or is that only half right? Considering the enemy, the old evil foe, are waging combat and making enemies within our body of faithful really options for the Bride of Christ?

Changing Your Side of the Relationship

Allow me one final *system's thought* on dealing with organizational conflict as it affects both the organization and also individual members. I mentioned it at the beginning of this section—you can only change *your half* of any relationship.

You can hope and prod, bully, threaten, and establish rules to attempt to change or humiliate your conflicted colleague. But the only way to resolve struggles harmoniously and effectively is to stop blaming *them* for the tension and conflict because of *your* perception of their error. Expending most of your emotional energy and resources trying to change those in opposition is a bad waste of precious energy. You can invite them to change, but the most fundamental change has to occur within yourself, within your spirit, with the establishment of *peace* within y*our* heart. When you change your heart, only accomplished by the power of the Holy Spirit of God at work, you then *become* the *gift of peace*. Your non-fearful, non-anxious presence becomes the *gift* for resolution of the conflict. (1 Corinthians 12:1-6)

This is accomplished through strengthening relationships, our relationship with Christ that he builds and matures through the Holy Spirit, and our relationship with our brother and sister in Christ, which the Spirit also facilitates.[12]

Finally, place the conflict in the space between you and your neighbor, understanding what issues and emotional baggage you each might be bringing to the table. Effectively *deal* with *your half* of the conflict; realize where *your heart* has become hardened, and ask the Lord to heal you. Receive God's peace in your own being. Wow, is that challenging! But that does require emotional and, I dare say, spiritual maturity.

In the spiritual realm of the Christian family of faith, that requires the presence and action of the Holy Spirit within Christ's Church and the brothers and sisters he died to save. And we do know God empowers some of God's flock to be prepared and gifted reconcilers and peacemakers.

Who is it, with the empowerment of the Holy Spirit, who can be facilitators of conflict resolution? That can be a challenging question for organizations such as religious denominations. At the Christian congregational level, this should be the task of the spiritual head, pastor or priest, with the congregation's board of directors or elders lifting up the pastor's arms and heart. If the local spiritual leader, or a member of the supporting board, is skilled in conflict resolution—and, I might add, spiritually mature—they can serve as the first line of therapy to suffering individuals caught in these troubling circumstances. I would also urge the consultation or even assistance of professional and credentialed counselors, either inside or better yet, outside of the congregation where available.

Occasionally in Christian faith communities, the pastor may not have those skills, or the pastor may, in fact, be a party in the conflict itself. Many faith bodies then have effective conflict resolution processes in place. They may have ecclesiastical authorities such as elected or appointed fellow clergy reconcilers, elected bishops, regional or national presidents, or executive leaders, coupled with boards of directors and governance. They may also have accessory ministries particularly skilled at conflict resolution to call on for assistance. I'll mention several of these momentarily.

These are enormous and complex responsibilities. The issues facing these leaders are organizational as well as faith-based. Therefore I believe good consultation with medical and counseling resources, and even legal input to complement the spiritual guidance, can assist to the edification of all sides of these conflicts.

An interesting and hopeful project within one faith community, the Lutheran Church—Missouri Synod (LCMS), entitled the Koinonia Project, might be a helpful model to share with the Church at large. The term *koinonia* is the Greek word for *fellowship*. While I am aware that several Christian denominations are undertaking similar efforts toward unity and fellowship, I will share the effort from my particular denomination, the LCMS, in that I know that project best.

As with many U.S.-based denominations during the last century in particular, the LCMS has been dealing with substantial conflict, culminating in a denominational schism in 1973 that split clergy, laity, families, seminary faculties, and denominational leadership.

After years of turmoil, much of which was passionate and public, the Synod-wide convention of 2007 mandated a task force, appointed by the board of directors and the Council of Presidents, who are regional ecclesiastical leaders, under the direction of the Synodical president, to focus on Synodical harmony toward mission and ministry. The hope and prayer was that we as a church body could move forward from this conflict in a Christ-centered and Scripturally based manner. In 2010 the task force suggested many possible strategies to deal with the Synod's "life together" under the goals of mercy, witness, and life together. The name chosen for this initiative was the *Koinonia Project*.

The Koinonia Project had a Scriptural theme from Ephesians 4:2-3:

> *"We pray the blessing of God as we bear 'with one another in love, eager to maintain the unity of the Spirit in the bond of peace.'"*

The project was designed to foster "theological decisions under the Word of God which we pray will strengthen our joint witness to the saving doctrine and bring greater unity to our practice of the same for the sake of God's people." This effort did not seek a new set of faith confessions, but it was to provide a greater understanding and renewed commitment to what we have inherited from our Christian forbearers as a denomination for the purpose of making our Gospel proclamation clear to everyone. "It does not seek compromise on the lowest common denominator, but a clear confession of the truth of God's Word and a salutary agreement as to how the doctrine can be put into practice."

The Koinonia Project realizes that *fellowship* is a grace-gift of God given to God's people in Jesus Christ. The project offers an opportunity for God's people to study the Word together because that is where God gives us the gift of *koinonia*. This time in the Word provides us with an opportunity for repentance of our sinful nature toward each other and before God, but also gives us an opportunity to focus on the need for theological dialogue under God's Word so that we might seek a greater *concord* in both doctrine and practice.

The Koinonia Project is not a political process or dialogue, as we have had much of that through this conflict dealing with our relationship struggles in our Synod, but rather a spiritual process centered on God's Word, Christ, and characterized by repentance and prayer, forgiveness, and charity toward one another; I would describe that as a *WE-oriented* process. Even as the Koinonia Project says, we have had lots of "adopt my resolution" or "vote my candidate in" type conversation leading to a "winning side and losing side" and hardening of hearts throughout our history.

In opposition to that win/lose characterization of our relationships in the LCMS, the Koinonia Project provides for a way for opposing sides to pause, sit, listen, and meet together so that specific objectives can be fostered:

1. Clarify the real *point* of contention.

2. Provide a clear statement of what we can *agree* on.

3. Provide a clear statement about what we *reject*.

4. Provide a statement of what we will *do* together.

This project clearly addresses the issues of remaining faithful to established doctrine and confessions, something that I believe is important to all sides, and still allows us as a church body to meet together to study, listen, communicate, *ally*, and work together to lessen conflict, seek unity, glorify God, and serve God's people.

The project provides a practical example of how this might be done. This example comes from the Northern Illinois District of the LCMS, a regional district encompassing Chicago and the northern reaches of the state of Illinois. Here is an outline of the process:

- Gather well-respected clergy with varying viewpoints and who are known to be able to *play in the same sandbox without throwing sand.*

- Be facilitated by a neutral person to help build relationships, study Scriptures, and develop statements of agreements and disagreements. Further determine where the clefts are between the sides.

- Reconvene and place the viewpoints in front of ecclesiastical leadership consultants, seminary faculties, and denominational theological specialists.

- Refine the statements of agreement and disagreement based on the above reviews, taking all comments into consideration.

- Expand the base of participants by referring the agreed-upon statement of the parameters of the controversy to additional Koinonia groups of clergy in the district, seeking their input.

- While the new Koinonia groups are meeting and working together, the original Koinonia group intentionally works on specific points of contention. For example, who might be admitted to receive the Lord's Supper in a given congregation, or what are the specific requirements to be considered *ordained* or serve as a qualified pastor in a congregation.

- Finally, when adequate time for discussion and study has been achieved to the group's satisfaction, the regional ecclesiastical supervisor, who would be the district president in this setting, will bring all together to develop a statement that the vast majority (75%) can agree to.

There is prayer, study, disarming discussion, thinking, listening, neutral facilitation, development of relationships, and finding points of conflict on which you can ally, hopefully building of trust and respect of opinions and, God-willing, fellowship, *koinonia*, that is unity in the Spirit.

This is just one example, and I suspect and pray you have something similar in your denomination. Yet we know there will still be individuals, often pastors, distressed by a sense of betrayal, disrespect, or lack of worth in their personal life and profession. They are sincerely hurting.

The skills and strategies for care of individuals distressed by denominational conflict or schism (and we've discussed better communication and listening skills, allying conflict resolution strategies, acknowledging deeply defining fears, and changing your half of the confrontation) are all helpful. But I believe the core of caring for these smitten brothers and sisters in Christ is to help them understand who they *are* in Christ, who they are in their Baptism, and what is their new value and worth as new Creations in Christ. (2 Corinthians 5:17) Jesus died for them. They cannot change, or work, or believe, or be faithful enough to *guarantee* being in God's family; it has been accomplished for them. Nor can they stumble, or falter, or err *too much* to be beyond God's grace, forgiveness, and love; it has been assured for them to eternity.

If you as a physician/counselor/therapist are capable of guiding this core spiritual understanding of being a child of God, then please make it a central part of your care. More often I believe this is where a wise and effective therapist partners *with* a pastor, priest, and a family of faith as the ones to bring God's full Word and Sacrament ministry into the healing process for these smitten individuals. This approach also reinforces the understanding of the human being as a unique body-soul creation of God, a whole being with the complete integration of physical, emotional, relational, vocational, and spiritual elements of life. All must be considered and treated in Christ to restore full health and wellbeing.

Despite the conflicts we humans bring into the life of the Church and God's family of faithful, we know the Lord's desire for us is to be part of "one body and one spirit, just as you were called to one hope when you were called; one Lord, one faith, one Baptism; one God and Father of all, who is over all and through all and in all." (Ephesians 4:4-6)

Spiritual and Personal Reconciliation through Confession and Forgiveness

The second major component, and quintessential component, for bringing peace into the hearts of those harmed by congregational and denominational conflict is to pursue *reconciliation* of personal and sin-based attitudes and behaviors within ourselves and with those with whom we are conflicted. The absolute need for reconciliation here is both personal and group confession and forgiveness or absolution. I have mentioned this as a grace-gift of God for dealing with fear and anxiety in Chapter Six under spiritual gifts, but let us explore this further as it might apply to the disagreements and disharmony within the group setting of our faith communities.

As we approach conflicted relationships within our Christian faith community, it is critical to remember that our first step in the healing process is the forgiveness of sins before whole healing can commence. We recall Matthew 9. Jesus steps into a boat and is going to Capernaum when he is brought a paralyzed man lying on a mat. Jesus sees the faith of the man's companions and says to the man, "Take heart, son: your sins are forgiven." As is often the case, Jesus is being critiqued by the some of the teachers of the law. Jesus knowingly responds, "Why do you entertain evil thoughts in your hearts? Which is easier: to say, 'Your sins are forgiven,' or to say, 'Get up and walk?' But I want you to know that the Son of Man has authority on earth to forgive sins." The paralyzed man's sins are forgiven and his paralysis healed, it appears, in that order.

So too it is in our group conflicts within the church. Are the conflict resolution skills and strategies we have discussed earlier in this chapter important and necessary, such as listening and clearly communicating, avoiding fundamental attribution errors, finding deeply seated core misperceptions, and working on changing our half of the relationship? Yes, of course they are necessary. However, confessing our sinfulness and our sin toward God and one another, and giving and receiving the same forgiveness that Christ died on the cross to earn for us, is essential. This involves confessing not just to each other, but also confessing to God and hearing God's forgiveness, which God stands with open arms to offer to us in Christ.

I turn to the thoughts of Ted Kober, founder and senior ambassador in an organization focused on conflict resolution and reconciliation in faith communities called Ambassadors of Reconciliation.[13] Mr. Kober reminds us of the guidance offered directly in God's Word. 1 Peter 2:24 tells us, "He himself bore our sins" in his body on the cross, so that we might die to sins and live for righteousness; "By his wounds you have been healed." In 2 Peter 1:3-4 we hear, "His divine power has given us everything we need for a godly life through our knowledge of him who called us by his own glory and goodness. Through these he has given us his very great and precious promises, so that through them you may participate in the divine nature, having escaped the corruption in the world caused by evil desires." And again, from Ephesians 4:32, "Be kind and compassionate to one another, forgiving each other, just as in Christ God forgave you." It is clear that the Holy Spirit is really the One empowering the healing.

Without the Spirit's softening of hardened hearts and leavening the process of peace, the reconciliation, trust, respectfulness, and restoration of rights to each side in the conflict will not be fully or lastingly accomplished. "Bear with each other and forgive one another if any of you has a grievance against someone. Forgive as the Lord forgave you. And over all these virtues put on love, which binds them all together in perfect unity. Let the peace of Christ rule in your hearts, since as members of one body you were called to peace. And be thankful." (Colossians 3:13-15)

There it is, as clearly and succinctly as can be stated, a Christian perspective and prescriptive for a heart at peace in a community of faith.

Additional Scripture for Peace

Since the scope of this book deals primarily with a Christian perspective on fear and anxiety ills, this is an appropriate point to search a bit more within the Holy Scriptures for guidance in the care of people suffering emotional and spiritual maladies due to church conflict. What do we know from the Bible about relational wellbeing in the family of faith? How are these truths supported by those who bring God's Word to us and who help us in a traditional and contemporary way to explain and defend the Scriptures?

Here are just a few reflections on Jesus' commands to us about living together. Each of you can supply many further examples:

- "'Love the Lord your God with all your heart and with all your soul and with all your strength and with all your mind'; and, 'Love your neighbor as yourself.'" (Luke 10:27) This forms the core of the teachings of the Law and prophets on life together in the Old Testament as well.

- Jesus gives two great commands at the Last Supper on the night he was betrayed referred to as Maundy Thursday, from the Latin *mandatum*. First, he says, "remember me" as he institutes the Sacrament of the Eucharist or Holy Communion in the sharing of his true body and blood—bread and wine—for the forgiveness of sins and building of faith in a new spiritual life. In his sacrificial and substitutionary death, he meets his followers' greatest needs. Second, he says, "A new commandment I give to you, that you love one another; just as I have loved you, you also are to love one another." (John 13:34) To demonstrate this love, in a show of humility that we should emulate, he washes his friends' feet. In this "command" he also calls us to love not just those with whom we find harmony and homogeny but also those with whom we are conflicted and those who don't even agree with us.

- Jesus addresses this concept of *competition* and *comparison* with his disciples James and John in Mark 10:35-45, as they ask to sit in places of honor as Jesus comes into his kingdom. These disciples, possibly even cousins of Jesus, wanted to keep the power in the *in-crowd*, in the *family*. This was a *me*-request for power and honor. The other fellows in the band of disciples were not so happy about being left out. Yet Jesus challenges them all, asking them if they are ready to suffer the same consequences he faces, and reminds them that it is God who chooses who receives the honors. He instructs them that whoever wants to sit in his eternal presence is called to a life of servanthood, of caring for and loving everyone—even if they're not "just like yourself." How much more loving our relationships could be within the family of faith if we heeded Christ's call to submit ourselves to each other, serve each other, be "*we's*" instead of "*me's*."

- Again, regarding leadership, the type Jesus shows (incidentally to those with whom he is very close) should be our model for leading his people: showing humility, servanthood, love, and care to the extreme for each other.

- Jesus was constantly addressing the *fundamental attribution errors* of the religious leaders of his day, who were in a constant mode of *catching* Jesus in error. There are more than 70 instances of Jesus interacting with religious leaders in the *in-crowd*. For example, Matthew 9:11: "When the Pharisees saw this, they asked his disciples, 'Why does your teacher eat with tax collectors and sinners [the *out-crowd*]?'" And how does Jesus respond? I'm only here for those who are perfect, healthy, agree with me? No. "On hearing this, Jesus said, 'It is not the healthy who need a doctor, but the sick. But go and learn what this means: 'I desire mercy, not sacrifice.'" (Matthew 9:12-13)

- Perhaps one of Jesus' greatest characteristics was that he listened well. He listened to his disciples, to those in need, to those who chose to be in conflict with him. Most importantly, he listened to the will of his Father. He continuously exemplified an intellectual curiosity about those with whom he was in relationship. Most often, they were not like him, not of his same *tribe*. Remember the woman at the well from John 4? This Samaritan woman was an outcast, a *nobody*. Jesus is curious, asks questions to establish a relationship, and then lifts her heart and spirit with *living water*. His communication, care, and sensitivity draw people into a relationship so that he can begin to help and heal.

- We know that sin itself, fear, and anxiety form the foundations of the emotional and spiritual distress resulting from denominational conflict. What do we know about anchoring to Jesus during these times of upheaval in our lives? "There is no fear in love. But perfect love [Jesus] drives out fear, because fear has to do with punishment. The one who fears is not made perfect in love. We love because he first loved us." (1 John 4:18)

You probably have many more examples of Jesus' mission and action to bring *all people* into his Father's kingdom. Most importantly, we have his death on the cross on behalf of all of us, to resolve our ultimate separation from God due to our self-interests and self-desires. Thanks be to God.

Takeaways

If you find yourself within a struggle bubbling up from congregational conflict as a clergy leader, board of governance member, lay member of a parish, or even caught within denominational turmoil, here are some medical and faith perspectives to bring to those challenging relationship circumstances:

Remember that this is a fear-based, relationship-connection challenge and a confession-forgiveness opportunity.

It is highly likely that this distress is deeply embedded enough that you may well need a professional counselor or experienced facilitator as well as a spiritual guide to walk through this relationship-connection struggle with you.

Be aware that Satan is lurking and looking for a place to establish a foothold. In your conflicted relationship, you are at risk of repeatedly going toward sundown in conflict and that is hurting both contentious parties. It is not healthy.

Forgive: honor and respect those with whom you are in conflict; assure them of their rights as children of the same Heavenly Father. Begin the entire healing process by first confessing your sins personally and as a group to God, receiving God's forgiveness, and then forgive each other as God has forgiven you.

Try to understand your relational and communication style. When you are expressing and sharing deep-seated feelings, are you *painting a picture,* or are you processing internally and then sharing *just the point?* What communication style does the one in conflict with you use? Are you listening, and do you feel you are being listened to?

This is an emotional, relational, and probably a vocational challenge to your body, mind, and soul. You may be experiencing physical distress as well as the emotional and spiritual signs and symptoms of fear.

Fear, most likely on both sides of the controversy, is at the foundation of the conflict. With the help of your counselor and spiritual guides, both of whom should be professionally trained, try to drill down into your emotional genetics (past history, response-to-stress style, etc.) to try to find the bedrock fear that might be creating turmoil within you and those with whom you are conflicted.

Remember that you can only change your half of the relationship-connection conflict. You can only affect *your heart,* which, through the power of the Holy Spirit, can be brought to *peace,* forming a truly *non-anxious presence* in the relationship. Then you become the gift of change, the vessel of carrying *healing.*

This is an *Emmaus journey* in your faith-walk. Look for Jesus to be there. He always is.

CHAPTER 11

ADDITIONAL FEARS, CHILDHOOD FEARS, AND GOOD GENERAL HEALTH

M any of you are probably familiar with the 2006 action thriller *Snakes on a Plane* starring one of my favorite actors Samuel L. Jackson. Okay, I admit I had trouble watching this one the third or fourth time. In 2016 passengers on a flight in Mexico actually experienced *a snake on a plane* dangling down from the overhead luggage compartment. Talk about checking off the boxes of what frightens us!

"For the Spirit God gave us does not make us timid, but gives us power, love and self-discipline." (2 Timothy 1:7)

There are many other fears within our culture beyond those related to health, of course. A list from the Gallup Poll in 2005 noted the most common fears for Americans included: terrorist attacks, spiders, death, being a failure, war, criminal or gang violence, being alone, the future, and nuclear war.

Add to this a list of what people have a "fear of," and the top ten list includes: flying, heights, clowns, intimacy, rejection, people, *snakes*, and driving. Other commonly identified fears include things from goblins and ghosts, to needles, to examinations, and public speaking. Please, add your own.

Yes, there seems to be an unending list of possible realities and uncertainties to which we as human beings can develop fear and anxiety. Many of these we learn from previous exposure, or inherited patterns of fear from parents, siblings, and even the media. All of these experiences get stored in our learning centers of the brain and then get integrated and adapted in some way into our ongoing responses and interactions.

I certainly recommend the medical and mental health therapies with which God has gifted us within this century, from psychotherapy, to medications, and holistic home remedies. But I believe that the base cause of fear is sin, and we are most deeply seeking not just the treatment of symptoms and signs of fear, but the action of God to heal the roots of fear. That requires the forgiveness of our sins and the strengthening of our faith in Christ by the power of the Holy Spirit.

In your fear and anxiety, walk with the Lord. As Jesus speaks to us today, "Therefore I tell you, do not worry about your life...how much more valuable you are than birds! Who of you by worrying can add a single hour to his life? Consider how the lilies grow. They do not labor or spin ... how much more will he clothe you, O you of little faith! ... Seek his kingdom ... Do not be afraid, little flock, for your Father has been pleased to give you the kingdom ... For where your treasure is, there your heart will also be." (Luke 12:22-34)

Ways to Cope with Fear in Children

Many of us rocked our youngsters to sleep in a favorite maple rocking chair handed down from generations, or perhaps from the IKEA store down the street. I fondly recall this loving pause each day with my middle child, and the confusion that her response evoked until I had the "aha" moment that came about when I was brave enough to ask, "What's scaring you, honey?" In her case, the fear came about by the shadows cast on the ceiling by a favorite night light, which I now admit, in retrospect, did look like—are you ready for it?—Uncle Fester of the Addams Family.

Most children, fortunately, grow out of the fear of monsters under the bed and shadows on the bedroom walls. But if you find your child is experiencing fears that limit his or her ability to function in daily life, it is time to talk to your physician. In the meantime, here are a few simple things that might assist you with your child:

- Talk openly about fears. Don't belittle your child or trivialize the problem. Assure your child that you are there to help and to listen. And then do be present and listen.

- Don't reinforce the fear. If your child is fearful of the big but friendly dog next door, don't go out of your way to avoid the dog. Instead, be a safe home base for your child as he or she gradually moves closer to the dog. Carefully, if things go well, encourage your child to draw near to the animal. Of course, if the dog is clearly a real danger, don't follow this strategy.

- Model positive behavior. Children learn by observing you. If you panic when confronted with the friendly hound, they too will panic. But if you demonstrate to your child how you respond when confronted with fear, you can positively show them how to deal with their own fear by your example.

Lifestyle Changes

I cannot overemphasize the importance of making some conscious lifestyle behavioral changes to treat all types of anxiety and fear. For the Christian, it begins with turning those fears and anxieties over to the Lord. Certainly, the grace-gifts offered through the Scriptures, prayer, your pastor, your faith community, and Christian counselors are the places to begin your healing journey. Here are a few additional whole health resources for you to consider:

- Keep physically active. Exercise is a marvelous means of releasing stress and tension. Develop routines that will allow you to be active daily. Begin slowly and then advance as your body will allow.

- Avoid stimulants like alcohol, or suppressants like sedatives.

- Don't smoke nicotine or marijuana, and substantially reduce caffeine and heavily caffeine-laden drinks (sodas, pops, and high-energy supplements), and also food with high-fructose additives, processed sugar, and refined wheat.

- Use relaxation techniques like meditation, yoga, and meditative prayer.

- Get adequate sleep, at least seven to eight hours nightly.

- Eat healthy, plenty of vegetables, whole grains, fruits, and fish. Try to limit red meat consumption to once a week if possible, which means four to five ounces, or about the size of a deck of cards. Eat one cup of beans (legumes) daily. Emphasize colorful vegetables, such as red, orange, yellow, or purple veggies. Make sure you know where your fish and produce are raised, preferring wild caught as opposed to farm raised and locally grown, organic, non-chemical laden fruits and veggies. Consume nuts for snacks.

- Tea is generally preferable to coffee, although there are some studies showing some benefit to coffee in prevention of diabetes. You need to assess your individual response to caffeine.

- If you have an upcoming appointment with a therapist, be prepared by being prompt and having a list of your medical and mental healthcare history, your current medications, and any associations, observations, and thoughts you might have on connecting your fears and anxieties to specific objects or circumstances.

- Stay on the regimen, medications, and mental health therapies outlined by your therapist. Note possible side effects and any other changes you experience while under care.

- Seek support groups of those suffering similar anxieties.

- When you are feeling overwhelmed by symptoms you correlate with your anxiety, try to break the cycle through a brisk walk or hobby to refocus away from your worries.

- Socialize; please do not let yourself become isolated from social interaction or caring relationships within family or friends.

Finally, there are many home remedies and alternative medications that have been used by some people in the treatment of their anxiety and fear, such as various herbs. The scientific and anecdotal reports are numerous, but far more research is needed to fully understand the risks and benefits of these therapies. I would urge you to consult your therapist directly with questions regarding these alternative treatments.

Never forget the power of prayer by you and those who love you. Sadly, I have met many people who are somehow ashamed of admitting to others that they have cancer, diabetes, chronic heart disease, lung disease, or a neurological or mental illness. I think you bless people by asking them for their prayers. God hears prayer! "The prayers of a righteous man are powerful and effective." (James 5:16) In fact, let me share with you a Scriptural mosaic on healing that we use often on our Grace Place Wellness Retreats:

> Leader (L): Those who suffer, God delivers in their suffering; he speaks to them in their affliction. (Job 36:15)
>
> **All: Hear my prayer, O Lord, let my cry for help come to you. Do not hide your face from me when I am in distress.** (Psalm 102:1-2)

L: All my longings lie open before you, O Lord; my sighing is not hidden from you. O Lord, do not forsake me; be not far from my, O my God. Come quickly to help me, O Lord my Savior. (Psalm 38:9, 21-22)

All: Is any one of you sick? He should call the elders of the church to pray over him and anoint him with oil in the name of the Lord. And the prayer offered in faith will make the sick person well; the Lord will raise him up. If he has sinned he will be forgiven. Therefore confess your sins to each other and pray for each other so that you may be healed. The prayer of a righteous man is powerful and effective. (James 5:14-15)

L: Jesus said, whoever comes to me, I will never drive away. (John 6:37)

All: Call upon me in the day of trouble; I will deliver you and your will honor me. (Psalm 50:15)

L: Trust in the Lord with all your heart and lean not on your own understanding. In all your ways acknowledge him, and he will make your paths straight. Do not be wise in your own eyes; fear the Lord and shun evil. (Proverbs 3:5-7)

All: This will bring health to your body and nourishment to your bones. (Proverbs 3:8)

CONCLUSION

The Health Coaching Team

There is an adage today in the world of healthcare that goes like this: you are your own, best, health advocate. The wisdom of this philosophy, from the Christian perspective, comes in our understanding of our *stewardship of our bodies, minds, and spirits* as "temples of the Holy Spirit." (1 Corinthians 6:19)

God has given us physical, emotional-intellectual-relational, vocational, fiscal, and spiritual elements of wellbeing, and invited us to be good stewards of these magnificent gifts. Again, I would urge you to glance at the Christian Wellness Wheel on the back of this book for reference. Even so, God has given us the most precious gift of the Son, Jesus, to restore our relationship with our Creator. The wages of sin, the fear and anxiety, separation, and illness, continuously threaten that stewardship in our earthly walk as saints and sinners. Only through God's Son and the power of the Holy Spirit is this stewardship possible. And we are not called to this stewardship all by ourselves. God gives us partners to carry on this thankful mission.

> *"And let us consider how we may spur one another on toward love and good deeds, not giving up meeting together, as some are in the habit of doing, but encouraging one another—and all the more as you see the Day approaching." (Hebrews 10:24-25)*

God *also* blesses each of us with additional complementary gifts of health *mentors* or *coaches* to lift our hearts and our minds in this stewardship journey. God provides pastors to bring Word and sacramental ministry to us in the care of our souls. God gives us skilled physicians to encourage the care of our physical ailments and guide us to best body practices. God provides wise counselors and mental health therapists to walk with us through the struggles of emotional turmoil that threaten the wellness, peace, and joy within our hearts. This is a team effort. Yet as stewards of

God's gifts, we each have responsibility to seek out the members of that team, access them when we need them, listen to and follow through on their coaching, and understand that the entire care team is headed by the Great Physician, Jesus Christ.

At certain times in this wellness journey we might need more coaching from one member of our care team. There are points in life where physical crises like cancer, heart disease, diabetes, neurological disorders, pain, or impending death might predominate as threats to wellbeing. We will expend increased energy to seek physical mentorship through those distresses. For others, the disorders of fear and excessive and repetitive anxiety such as phobias, obsessive-compulsive behavior, stress due to traumatic circumstances, and even prolonged depression or polar swings in our moods may wreak havoc with our thoughts and feelings. At this time the care team leader may be an experienced and compassionate mental health therapist. And occasionally our physical ailments will create enough anxiety that we additionally might need the assistance of mental health as well as faith advocates. We will seek mental health mentors and pastors to amplify the care team and support us through these challenges.

Sadly, in the noise, disruption, and tumult of disease, we may tend to forget about the empowering, consistent whisper of God's presence in Jesus in our lives. I would suggest to you that during all challenges to health, those of body, mind, and spirit, you need the coaching of your spiritual mentors, your pastors, and your faith community that invite you to God's gifts of grace. They will speak to you God's powerful Word, and they can lift you up before God's throne of mercy.

Thanks be to God! The healing of our fear and anxiety, the repairing of our diseased bodies, the calming of our troubled minds, and the peace within our hearts are assured, immediately, gradually, or ultimately, because God loves us enough to send Jesus. Our Savior removes the sting of fear and death, and through our reconciliation with God's family, Christ gives us the courageous energy to deal with fear so that it no longer consumes us.

Jesus' death and resurrection restores our right to come to God as beloved children, appropriately fearing and revering God's power to judge and to heal all of creation. God is merciful, and God is filled with compassion and love.

Through Christ, even in the depth of our fear and anxiety, we are called to remember and trust God's promise, "And surely I am with you always, to the very end of the age." (Matthew 28:20)

Jesus brings us wellness. Jesus brings us a heart at peace.

APPENDIX

HISTORICAL USE OF THE WORD ANXIETY

NEUROCHEMISTRY OF STRESS, FEAR, AND ANXIETY

DSM-5

GENERAL ANXIETY DISORDER

PANIC DISORDER/PANIC ATTACKS

PHOBIAS

POST-TRAUMATIC STRESS DISORDER

OBSESSIVE-COMPULSIVE DISORDER

DEPRESSION

BIPOLAR DISORDER

PAINTER/POINTER SCALE

WORD-SATURATED MEDITATIVE PRAYER

This is not meant to be a complete textbook on all mental health disorders that affect humankind. I do wish to focus on the most common fear-based mental illnesses facing our culture, beginning with some background on the word anxiety and a deeper look into the neurochemistry of fear and anxiety.

The appendix also contains background information on the organization of the Diagnostic and Statistical Manual of Mental Disorders (DSM-5). It is important to recognize the way mental health therapists and researchers classify and study mental illness. Subsequent sections also provide basic summaries of a variety of classified mental health disorders that have fear or anxiety as a common component of the disease. This includes general anxiety disorder along with a variety of anxiety disorders (agoraphobia, anxiety due to medical conditions, social anxiety disorder, substance-induced anxiety disorder, separation anxiety disorder in children, other specific or unspecified anxiety disorders, panic attacks, phobias, post-traumatic stress disorder, obsessive-compulsive disorder, depressive disorders, and bipolar disorders).

Again, this information is not to be meant to be a substitute for discussing all mental health concerns with your physician, therapist, and pastor. Please seek help for any emotional, behavioral, mental, and physical concerns disrupting your life with your healthcare team.

HISTORICAL USE OF THE WORD ANXIETY

The historical use of the word *anxiety* goes all the way back to Greek and Roman physicians and philosophers. In fact, the physicians of Jesus' time, perhaps even St. Luke the physician who undoubtedly was aware of contemporary medical concepts, identify anxiety both as a disorder of the spirit and the body. Let me just provide a bit more historical perspective on *anxiety* as you might appreciate how this applies to the ways we address and understand anxiety from a spiritual, physical, diagnostic, and therapeutic approach to mental wellbeing.

We pick up this story in the writings of the Hippocratic Corpus (*ca.* 460 BC to the first and second centuries AD, written by the disciples of Hippocrates, the father of modern medicine), which describe a man with an anxiety disorder called a *phobia*. The man became terrified every time he heard a flute played at night—but not during the day, just at night! We see the ancient Epicurean and Stoic philosophers prescribing techniques to free patients from anxiety not dissimilar to current cognitive therapy. Cicero (108 BC to 43 BC) describes affliction (*molestia*), worry (*solicitudo*), and anxiety (angor) in his *Tusculan Disputations*. He made the connection of a troubled mind or heart and a diseased body. In this text anxiety is beginning to be recognized as an actual medical illness associated with the body, but also involving another component of the human being, the mind or spirit.

In his work *Of Peace of Mind*, the Stoic philosopher Seneca (4 BC to AD 65) noted that the fear of death was the main cognition preventing us from enjoying a carefree life. Seneca's writings anticipate the further psychological developments by Kierkegaard, Heidegger, and the existentialists of the last two centuries.

Interestingly, for unknown reasons, there is a long interval between classical antiquity and the 19th century where we don't commonly see the word *anxiety* in usage, although illnesses like melancholia, panic attacks, and generalized anxiety disorder encompass the *panophobias* of the 18th century.[14] However, there is a long interval of time in the Dark Ages where we do not see much use of this concept of anxiety as a specific illness.

Finally, in the late 19th and 20th centuries, there is a rapid expansion of the description, etiology, and therapies for mental illness, particularly anxiety, developed by Sigmund Freud, Carl Jung, Kierkegaard, Erikson, and a host of other physicians. This all culminates in the development in 1952 of the first comprehensive collection of mental health disorders, known as the Diagnostic and Statistical Manual of Mental Health Disorders (DSM-I). In DSM-I the "chief characteristic of the psychoneurotic disorders was *anxiety* which might be directly felt and expressed or which might be unconsciously and automatically controlled by the utilization of various psychological defense mechanisms (depression, conversion, displacement, etc.)."

The diagnostic characteristics and therapeutic models have been successively advanced over the next 60 years through the additions of such diagnoses as panic disorders, generalized anxiety disorder, and post-traumatic stress disorder, bringing us in 2013 to the Diagnostic and Statistical Manual of Mental Disorders, Fifth Edition (DSM-5). The DSM-5 is the standard classification of mental health disorders used by mental health professionals, including counselors and therapists of all backgrounds. DSM-5 has three major components: the diagnostic classification of illness, the diagnostic criteria sets, and the descriptive text for the specific mental illness. Also, DSM-5 has provided the major contribution of grouping anxiety disorders into three general spectra (anxiety, obsessive-compulsive disorders (OCD), and trauma- and stressor-related disorders) based on sharing common features and grouping developmentally connected disorders in the same chapters.

The current DSM-5, although finally completed in 2013, accurately reflects thoughts and therapies extending back over 2,000 years in the descriptions, causes, and treatments of disorders of the mind and human spirit as it interacts with the human body.

Additionally, and importantly, since we are dealing with insurance coverage for mental health disorders, each diagnosis in the DSM-5 has a diagnostic code used to collect data and provide billing. All U.S. healthcare providers use the same coding system, the International Classification of Diseases, Ninth Edition, Clinical Modification (ICD-9-CM), which applies to all illness, mental or physical.

Why is this long history lesson on anxiety pertinent to a discussion of fear, particularly from the Christian perspective? Some in our faith community might struggle with the idea of anxiety as a real disorder of the spirit, as the word is not used in some of the classic translations of Scripture, such as the original King James Version. I believe that might be so because at the time of the translation, the term *anxiety* was not commonly used. Yet, the concept of this *spirit-troubling* and *physically reactionary* emotion is surely evident. In more recent translations, the term *anxiety* is evident in both the Old Testament and the New, including the New International Version, English Standard Version, Amplified Bible, and New King James Version.

NEUROCHEMISTRY OF STRESS, FEAR, AND ANXIETY

Let me share some of the more recent advances in our medical understanding of the biochemical pathways that seem to be involved in the emotions of fear and anxiety, and how these discoveries might help us proceed with medical/psychological therapies to treat these disorders.

HPA-Axis

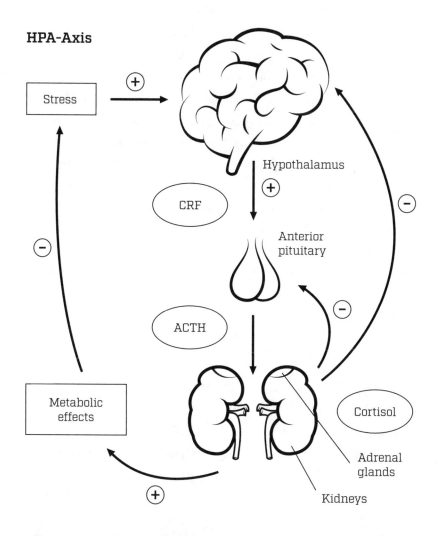

Here's a brief look at the neurochemistry of stress, fear, and anxiety. The human response to stress and fear involves, again, the *HPA-axis* (the hypothalamus and pituitary glands in the brain and their neuron, or nerve, wiring, coupled with secretions released into the blood stream, and impacting the adrenal glands that sit on top of the kidneys), and somatic cells throughout our body (liver, GI tract, muscles, nerves, kidneys, heart, to name a few). There are two peptide hormones, corticotrophin-releasing hormone (CRH) and arginine-vasopressin (AVP), that are released by the hypothalamus in the center of the brain in response to stress or fear.

CRH is sent to the pituitary gland, sitting at the bottom middle of our brain, and it causes the pituitary to release the adrenocorticotropic hormone (ACTH) from its posterior portion. ACTH causes the increased production of corticosteroids including cortisol by the outer cortex of the adrenal gland along with dehydroepiandrosterone (DHEA). Cortisol is the primary hormone that regulates our responses to stress and fear. DHEA is what we call a glucocorticoid receptor antagonist—it prevents excessive inflammation, but it also tends to protect the neurological organs and machinery from the damaging effects of cortisol, particularly the hippocampus. At the same time, the hypothalamus causes activation of the noradrenergic neurons of the locus caeruleas/norepinephrine (LC/NE) system in the brain. That LC/NE system is mostly responsible for the fight-or-flight response by driving the secretion of epinephrine and norepinephrine from the middle portion of the adrenal glands. That medullary or middle part of the adrenal gland is the main secreting organ of the sympathetic nervous system.

Norepinephrine and epinephrine increase our heart rate and blood pressure, preparing our body to fight or flee.

Cortisol proceeds to numerous target cells in our liver's glucose-regulating systems, gastrointestinal, and immune cells, fat and protein cells, and insulin-receptor sites in our cells, preparing us to respond to stresses and fears.

DHEA, among other effects, increases our testosterone to strengthen our muscular response to stress and fear and to modify the effects of cortisol on our cells.

Additionally, the hypothalamus releases AVP, which directly impacts our kidneys by causing them to reabsorb water, and causes our arteries to constrict and thereby increase our blood pressure, all in preparation for the fight-or-flight response. As these hormones, CRH and AVP, float around our body, they also provide feedback regulation to the HPA-axis, causing it to be stimulated more or quieted down.

Cortisol's additional purpose is to restore balance following our body's exposure to stress. Therefore, beyond the chemical or metabolic effects, cortisol also affects ion transport, our immune response, and even our memory. It carefully regulates our blood sugar levels by both increasing sugar production by our body and at the same time increasing the usage of sugar in our liver.

Cortisol also regulates our ions, or sodium and potassium, and therefore balances our body's pH (acid-base levels), bringing it back into equilibrium after stressful events.

I mentioned that cortisol affects our immune system. It does so by regulating the number and responsiveness of the so-called T-cells, or T-lymphocytic cells. It also stifles inflammation by inhibiting the release of histamine. So when cortisol levels remain high for a long time, it may make people in a constant state of fear or anxiety highly vulnerable to infection, by bathing the immune cells in products that basically tell them to stop fighting the attack.

Finally, cortisol can affect memory and cognition. The hippocampus is a region of the brain where memories seem to be stored. The hippocampus contains many cortisol-receptor cells. When cortisol levels remain high, as in chronic anxiety and stress, the hippocampus can atrophy or shrink in size.

DIAGNOSTIC AND STATISTICAL MANUAL OF MENTAL DISORDERS: DSM-5

DSM-5 was completed in 2013, the latest of five efforts to classify and describe mental health disorders. This manual revised the previous effort (DSM-4) from the 1990s, precipitated by the many scientific and therapeutic advances in recent years.

As you can see from the table of contents listed below, new classifications are based on how various conditions relate to one another and the occurrence of mental health disorders across a lifespan. Both those perspectives influence mental healthcare. The primary purpose of the update is to help clinicians make more accurate and consistent diagnoses and to help researchers better study the illnesses and the way they interrelate.

Four hundred experts from 13 countries, representing the disciplines of psychiatry, psychology, neurology, pediatrics, primary care, epidemiology, research methodology, and statistics participated in this reclassification process. Representatives from the World Health Organization, National Institutes of Health, and American Psychiatric Association all worked together to create the DSM-5, which also certainly included input from the international community.

Research in the past two decades has rapidly expanded our understanding of the underlying vulnerability to illnesses, such as what genetic, biochemical, psychologic, physiological, or spiritual propensities we possess that might make us susceptible or likely to develop a mental illness, as well as symptom characteristics of these illnesses. The research has centered on how the brain functions and the various influences of genetics and environment on the subsequent display of mental disorders. We understand that many illnesses share common features and are related even across larger disorder groups. Better understanding leads to better therapy.

Furthermore, DSM-5 is organized in a sequence across the developmental lifespan. Therefore even within one disorder category, the discussion first focuses on illness typically diagnosed in childhood, then adolescence, then adulthood, and finally in later life.

The various chapters are organized to show both the differences and similarities across disorders. There are a few newer classification disorders, for example, neurodevelopmental disorders. This category now includes the autism spectrum, intellectual developmental disorders, attention-deficit/hyperactivity disorder, and tic disorders. The new chapter on substance-related illnesses is now entitled "Substance Use and Addictive Disorders" and even includes gambling disorder as its own behavioral addiction, and so on.

Our new scientific understandings of principal features of certain illnesses have also contributed to reclassification of some disorders. As we now understand that obsessive-compulsive disorder involves distinct neurocircuits, it and several other related illnesses are placed in their own category rather than being lumped into anxiety disorders. In the same manner, mood disorders are now divided into two separate designations as bipolar disorders and depressive disorders.

Here is the complete listing of DSM-5 chapters:

- Neurodevelopmental Disorders
- Schizophrenia Spectrum and Other Psychotic Disorders
- Bipolar and Related Disorders
- Depressive Disorders
- Anxiety Disorders
- Obsessive-Compulsive and Related Disorders
- Trauma- and Stressor-Related Disorders
- Dissociative Disorders

- Somatic Symptom Disorders
- Wake Disorders
- Sexual Dysfunctions
- Gender Dysphoria
- Disruptive, Impulse Control, and Conduct Disorders
- Substance Use and Addictive Disorders
- Neurocognitive Disorders
- Personality Disorders
- Paraphilic Disorders
- Other Disorders

The most detailed version of the classifications can be found online at www.psychiatry.org/dsm5. The illnesses that follow are highlighted because they are more common. However, complete descriptions and therapeutic considerations can be found on the Internet from very trustworthy sources, including the following:

- See www.psychiatry.org/dsm5 for descriptions of DSM-5 classifications.

- The Mayo Clinic: www.mayoclinic.org. Enter the specific mental disorder that you wish to explore.

- National Institutes of Mental Health: www.nimh.nih.gov. Enter the specific mental disorder that you wish to explore.

- American Psychiatric Association Classifications: www.psychiatry.org. Enter "DSM" to find information.

GENERAL ANXIETY DISORDER (GAD)
(DSM-5 Category: Anxiety Disorders)

As noted in Chapter 3, GAD is characterized by an exaggerated anxiety and worry about everything in life that, if untreated, leads to substantial dysfunction with daily life, including school, work, social activities, and relationships.

In DSM-5, anxiety disorders include:

- Generalized anxiety disorder (GAD)
- Separation anxiety disorder
- Selective mutism
- Specific phobia
- Social anxiety disorder (social phobia)
- Panic attack (specifier)
- Agoraphobia
- Substance/medication-induced anxiety disorder
- Anxiety disorder due to another medical condition
- Other specified anxiety disorder
- Unspecified anxiety disorder

I'll review a few of these most common anxiety disorders. General anxiety disorder is associated with physical symptoms that include:

- Excessive and ongoing worry
- An unrealistic view of challenges and stresses
- General restlessness or a feeling of being constantly on edge
- Irritability
- Muscle tension or spasm

- Headaches

- Excessive sweating

- Trouble concentrating

- Sense of having to run to the bathroom continuously

- Fatigue

- Trembling in body or extremities

- Shortness of breath

- Sleeplessness, or early waking with inability to fall back asleep

People with GAD may also have panic disorders or experience phobias.

The cause of GAD is not fully understood, but it appears that several factors are common, including family genetics, brain chemistry, and perhaps even environmental influences. The portions of the brain associated with thinking and emotions may not run efficiently or the circuits might not be in synchronization. Furthermore, traumatic events like the death of a loved one or physical or emotional trauma may trigger GAD. Finally, if a person is habituated or addicted to certain substances like nicotine, marijuana, alcohol, or even caffeine, these can worsen general anxiety.

Symptoms of GAD can vary but can include:

- Continuous worry about concerns that is out of proportion to the actual impact of the event

- Inability to let go of a worry

- Inability to relax

- Difficulty concentrating

- Worrying about worrying

- Distress about making decisions, always fearing you will make the wrong decision

- Carrying every possible option to its possible negative conclusion

- Flashing in your mind every possible negative conclusion
- Inability to handle uncertainty or indecisiveness

There are specific symptoms of GAD in children or teenagers. Youth can have excessive worry about:

- Performance in sports or school work
- Punctuality
- Potential catastrophic events

Children or teens with GAD may also experience:

- Trouble fitting in with the crowd
- Being a perfectionist
- Constantly redoing tasks trying to achieve perfection
- Lack of confidence
- Spending excessive time on homework or to perfect a sport
- Always trying to gain acceptance or approval from parents or friends
- Requiring lots of reassurance about performance

When Should You Seek Professional Help?

Sometimes it is tough to figure out the point when you or your child needs medical assistance with anxiety. Here are a few helpful guidelines from the staff at Mayo Clinic:

- When worry is interfering with your work, school, or relationships
- When you feel depressed, are trying to self-medicate with alcohol or other drugs, or are experiencing other mental health disorders like panic attacks or phobias
- If you or your child are experiencing suicidal thoughts, this is an emergency and you need to seek treatment immediately. If you

suspect suicidal thoughts in your child, it is best to ask them about them and follow up with a physician or counselor.

Are there some risk factors to developing GAD?

- Genetics: GAD may run in families.
- Personality: a person who is timid or who avoids anything dangerous might be more prone to GAD.
- Being female: women are diagnosed with GAD more often than men.

There are several significant complications of GAD if not treated promptly or adequately:

- Sleep disturbance
- Debilitating fatigue
- Impaired performance
- Inability to concentrate

GAD can also worsen other mental or physical health disorders:

- Depression
- Substance abuse
- Insomnia
- GI symptoms of diarrhea or constipation
- Headaches
- Heart issues like hypertension, angina, palpitations

Who should you see if you suspect you have GAD? First, a discussion with your primary care physician will be helpful. He or she can help assess whether this is an anxiety disorder or whether there are underlying physical/medical issues that could be causing your symptoms, for example, gastrointestinal disorders, heart disease, diabetes, thyroid disease, or others. If you are physically okay, then your physician should refer you to a certified and licensed psychologist or psychiatrist. You may certainly also seek spiritual guidance through your pastor as a part of the total care of your fear and anxiety, including participating in the spiritual resources discussed in Chapter Five. However, unless your pastor is also a licensed psychologist or psychiatrist, the medical and mental healthcare of GAD should include a referral to one of these highly trained and certified therapists.

The therapist may also require you to have a thorough physical done including blood and urine tests. They may also suggest a psychological questionnaire to help make an accurate psychological diagnosis. You may hear or see your therapist use the DSM-5 (Diagnostic and Statistical Manual of Mental Disorders from the American Psychiatric Association) criteria to classify your specific anxiety state as generalized anxiety disorder. This helps the doctor differentiate problems such as depression, post-traumatic stress disorder (PTSD), substance abuse, panic disorder, and phobias.

The treatment of GAD has been touched on earlier in this book, but generally uses a combination of therapies including psychotherapy (CBT or MBT/ACT); medications such as antidepressants like SSRIs (selective serotonin reuptake inhibitors) or SNRIs (serotonin norepinephrine reuptake inhibitors); buspirone; or benzodiazepines, which are sedatives like alprazolam, chlordiazepoxide, diazepam, or lorazepam. There are several other anxiety disorders that bear very similar characteristics to GAD and therapists sometimes find it helpful to place them in their own category to assist in therapy. Therapies may be similar to that for GAD but more tailored or specified depending on the specific classification of the anxiety stressor.

- Agoraphobia: in this disorder you fear and even avoid situations or places that might cause you to panic or feel helpless, trapped, or embarrassed.

- Anxiety disorder due to medical conditions: a physical health issue may directly cause anxiety or a helpless feeling, which often occurs in patients with cancer, heart disease, diabetes, lung disease (COPD), kidney disease, thyroid disorders like hyperthyroidism, irritable bowel disorder or inflammatory bowel disease (Crohn's or ulcerative colitis), or rare endocrine tumors that produce "fight-or-flight" hormones.

- Selective mutism: found in children, this disorder causes children to avoid speaking in certain social situations like school even though they may feel safe to speak at home around family.

- Separation anxiety disorder: although all children have some fear and anxiety when separated from parents or family to some extent, especially in the first year or two of life, this disorder finds children showing excessive anxiety for the child's developmental level and might be caused by separation from anyone with parental roles.

- Social anxiety disorder (also called social phobia) involves a high level of anxiety, fear and avoidance in social situations resulting from feelings of embarrassment or self-consciousness, especially about being viewed negatively, or constantly being judged by others.

- Specific phobias: I will cover these under the "Phobias" section of this appendix.

- Substance-induced anxiety disorder: this disorder comes about due to abusing drugs, taking a variety of medications, withdrawal from illicit drugs or medication, and being exposed to toxins.

- Other specified or unspecified anxieties or phobias that don't meet the exact criteria for those mentioned above, but still produce disruption in life.

Additional reading resources:

- WebMD: www.webmd.com. See the "Anxiety & Panic Disorders Health Center" page.

- Mayo Clinic: www.mayoclinic.org. See the "Generalized Anxiety Disorder" page.

- The National Institute of Mental Health: www.nimh.nih.gov. See the "Generalized Anxiety Disorder (GAD): When Worry Gets Out of Control" page.

- Mayo Clinic: www.mayoclinic.org. See the "Anxiety" page.

PANIC DISORDER/PANIC ATTACKS
(DSM-5 Category: Anxiety Disorders)

A panic attack is a sudden intense fear that leads to severe physical reactions, but it occurs when there is no apparent cause or real danger. These attacks can be very infrequent, perhaps occurring only once or twice in a lifetime and associated with a stressful situation. The fear is very real, however, and you may experience thinking you are totally losing control, experiencing a heart attack, or even dying. Unfortunately some people may experience these episodes of fear more frequently and without warning.

These panic episodes themselves are not life-threatening, but the associated fright may substantially affect the quality of your life.

Panic attacks generally begin very suddenly without warning. The physical symptoms like chest pain or sweating peak quickly and then dissipate, but you may feel extremely fatigued afterward.

Here are a few common symptoms associated with panic attacks:

- Fear of impending death
- Chest pain or pounding
- Sweating
- Trembling
- Shortness of breath
- Chills
- Hot flashes
- GI distress including nausea and abdominal cramps
- Headache
- Dizziness
- Tingling of feet and hands

Probably one of the most crippling aspects of panic attacks is that you fear another attack, and although not always sure what caused the initial episode, you may start avoiding certain situations altogether in the hopes of preventing the panic.

These episodes are extremely difficult to treat yourself, so it is very important to seek medical or mental health expertise to help you deal with these frightening experiences.

Furthermore, since panic attack symptoms are so similar to other medical conditions, it is important for your health and peace of mind to be thoroughly evaluated.

There appear to be some families in which this disorder may affect several members. We know that major stresses and losses in life can trigger episodes, and some people whose temperament is very sensitive may be more prone to panic attacks.

Panic attack symptoms can often start in late teens or early adulthood, and tend to be more common in women, although men are not immune. There are a few major risk factors to consider:

- Family history
- Major stresses like the loss or serious illness of a loved one
- Serious traumatic events like a major accident or sexual assault
- Childhood history of sexual abuse
- Divorce or loss of baby or child
- Intense use of nicotine, caffeine, or similar stimulants

There is great need to treat these panic disorders early, or risk developing specific phobias that limit quality of life, or frequent unnecessary trips to the emergency room for symptoms. If untreated, there also appears to be an increased risk of depression, more serious psychiatric illness, or even suicide. Finally, there is also an increased risk of developing self-medication abuses like alcohol or drugs, as well as substantial financial risk.

Since symptoms of panic attack and physical illness can be so similar, your physician may want to begin with a thorough medical exam including blood work, heart studies, or X-rays. He or she will want to exclude endocrine disease like thyroid disorders or diabetes. Certainly he or she will want to do a thorough psychologic evaluation, exploring your stresses, fears, past history, and relationships. He or she may choose to do some written psychological questionnaires as well. Most probably, they will use the DSM-5 (see previous discussion on GAD) looking for the following criteria:

- Are your attacks frequent and unexpected?

- Do you follow an attack with a month or more of continued worry or fear about experiencing another episode of panic?

- Your attacks are not caused by stimulants, drugs, or other medical causes (thyroid/heart/lung disease), and you do not have other mental health issues like phobias or obsessive-compulsive disorder (OCD).

It is important to remember that excellent treatments for panic attacks exist. Therefore earlier diagnosis and treatment are critical to healing. Although we have talked about these for other mental health disorders, the same general treatment resources are useful for panic attacks:

- Psychotherapy: this should always be the first line of treatment.

- Medications: SSRIs, SNRIs, and benzodiazepine sedatives can be useful. However, dependency from long-term use is always a concern and the use of these medications should always be thoroughly supervised by your therapist.

- Occasionally medications may seem to work for a while and then lose effectiveness, so your therapist may choose to change medications or even combine medications to achieve better results. All of these medications are powerful and may not be recommended in certain situations like pregnancy; all may have substantial side effects. Any unusual symptoms while taking these medicines should be discussed with your therapist.

Just a few general suggestions:

- Stay on your medications and keep your appointments for follow-up.

- Stick to your treatment plan.

- Find a support group; this is hugely important.

- Avoid stimulants like caffeine, nicotine, and alcohol.

- Find and practice relaxation techniques like yoga, stretching, or progressive muscle relaxation where you are tensing the then relaxing alternating muscle groups.

- Exercise regularly and eat nutritiously.

- Get adequate sleep, at least seven to eight hours per night.

Further reading can be found online by searching "Panic Attacks" and/or "Panic Disorders" at:

www.mayoclinic.org

www.lifescript.com

www.webmd.com

PHOBIAS
(DSM-5 Category: Anxiety Disorders)

A phobia is an overwhelming and unreasonable fear of a situation or an object that poses very little threat but still produces anxiety and avoidance. Phobia is not brief but rather long-lasting. It produces intense physical and emotional reactions, and generally severely limits your ability to function at work or in a social setting.

Not all phobias are of the severity that they need treatment. However, when the fear provoked by a specific individual, object, or social setting interferes with daily life, it should be treated.

There are three major categories of phobias:

Specific phobias: This is characterized by irrational and persistent fear of objects or circumstances out of proportion to the actual risk or danger. The most common specific phobias include fear of insects or other animals (dogs, snakes, spiders); nature (storms or heights); situations (airplanes or enclosed spaces); blood or injections; physicians; injuries; or other things (clowns or loud noises).

Social phobias: This is more than simple shyness. It generally involves rather severe self-consciousness coupled with fear of public humiliation. The person fears being rejected, receiving negative evaluation, or even offending others.

Fear of open spaces (agoraphobia): In agoraphobia, the person fears being in an actual or anticipated situation, like being in a crowded space, having to use public transportation, being in confined spaces, standing in a line in a crowd, or being away from home alone. The fear comes from being afraid that there is no easy source of help, or no easy way to escape. Agoraphobia often develops after having a panic attack in a certain situation and then developing constant fear of the same situation. Occasionally the person is unable to even leave home.

No matter which phobia precipitates the reaction, the patient feels uncontrollable panic and terror when exposed to the source of the fear. Sufferers all fear that they need to do whatever is possible to avoid that object or situation at all cost. They cannot function, and when in that circumstance, they develop the physical signs and symptoms as with other fear disorders like sweating, palpitations, rapid heartbeat, trouble breathing, and panic. Phobias cannot be diagnosed through a specific lab test. Rather, phobias are diagnosed through a detailed clinical interview and use of DSM-5 criteria. As with other disorders related to fear, a full social, medical, and psychiatric history and physical exam are important.

Here are the major criteria for diagnosing specific phobias:

- Intense fear triggered by an object or situation, like snakes, flying, or storms
- An immediate physical anxiety response when confronted with the object of fear
- Fear out of proportion to the risk
- Avoidance behavior from the object or situation causing the fear
- Significant social distress due to the fear
- Persistent phobia and avoidance lasting greater than six months

Seek medical help when these fears begin to seriously disrupt your life. If phobias are left untreated, the long-term problems can include social isolation, depression, substance abuse, and even suicide.

The treatment for phobias can be extremely effective and help return the sufferer to functional living. The therapy, as in other fear disorders, includes:

Psychotherapy

- Desensitization therapy (exposure therapy) focuses on gradually exposing you repeatedly to the cause of your phobia in a safe, controlled environment. For example, if you fear elevators, your therapist will lead you through stages of first thinking about elevators, then looking at pictures of elevators, then going near an elevator, stepping into an elevator, and then, finally, riding up one floor.

- Cognitive behavioral therapy, which is fully discussed in the "Bipolar Disorder" section of this appendix.

Medications

- Beta blockers: Medications that block the stimulating effects of adrenaline like increased heart rate, blood pressure elevation, or shakiness of limbs. They have a short-term effect and can be used just before facing a fearful situation like public speaking or a musical performance.

- Antidepressants: SSRIs that selectively inhibit the uptake of serotonin, which is a neurotransmitter in the brain that is felt to influence moods.

- Sedatives: Benzodiazepines help you to relax by reducing the amount of anxiety that you feel. They can be very addictive so are to be used cautiously and for a limited time.

Further reading can be found online by searching "Phobias" at:

www.mayoclinic.org

www.kidshealth.org

www.healthline.com

www.mentalhealthamerica.net

POST-TRAUMATIC STRESS DISORDER
(DSM-5 Category: Trauma- and Stressor-Related Disorders)

There are many trauma and stressor-related illnesses now classified in the DSM-5 system. They include:

- Reactive attachment disorder
- Disinhibited social engagement disorder
- Post-traumatic stress disorder
- Acute Stress disorder
- Adjustment disorders
- Other specified trauma- and stressor-related disorders
- Unspecified trauma- and stressor-related disorder

Those of us with memories of the Korean and Vietnam Wars, the Oklahoma City bombing, the 9/11 World Trade Center attack, and all of the Gulf strife in the last 50 years are very familiar with the term post-traumatic stress disorder (PTSD), also now commonly known as PTS. Indeed, this psychological response to trauma has been around probably since Cain slew Abel, but we have found a four-letter abbreviation to put a handle on the disorder.

PTSD (PTS) results in a series of emotional and physical reactions to a witnessed or experienced traumatic event. These reactions may begin anywhere from three months to years after the event. Obviously, many types of events from war or torture, sexual abuse, auto accidents, or natural disasters can cause a person to fear a threat to personal life or wellbeing. PSTD can follow any of these fears.

The following symptoms are common in people who suffer from PTSD:

- Physical pain: PTSD may begin with headaches or migraines, fatigue, digestive distress, dizziness, chest pain, or shortness of breath.

- Nightmares and flashbacks: This is a common symptom characteristic of PTSD. This is a re-experiencing of the feared trauma. It can occur in dreams or even in the awakened state. It is common in both adults and children. It can occur with fear of leaving home or lead to major disturbances like insomnia.

- Anxiety and depression: phobias of people, situations, or events in PTSD sufferers can lead to uncontrollable anxiety and depression.

- Withdrawal: both adults and children with PTSD who have previously been socially stable may suddenly lose interest in enjoyable activities or hobbies, avoid friends, or seek out risky behavior, drug or alcohol dependency, or thrill seeking.

- Avoidance: Sufferers of PTSD may avoid any physical or mental stimuli that remind them of a traumatic or dangerous event. After a car accident, a PTSD-affected person may avoid driving or even traveling in cars.

- Repression: PTSD sufferers may intentionally block memories of past traumatic events or people. They may even go as far as destroying pictures, messages, or memorabilia associated with these traumatic events. They may try to throw themselves into their work or even other relationships.

- Emotional numbing: By numbing feelings, PTSD sufferers try to avoid the pain of a memory. However, they may also gradually withdraw and isolate themselves from all friends and social settings.

- Hyper-arousal: PTSD patients may have "nerves" or the jitters so severe that they cannot relax. They may always feel "on edge."

- Irritability: PTSD sufferers can be so fearful and paranoid that they are constantly irritable, indecisive, sleepless, and unable to focus on work or relationships.

- Shame and guilt: PTSD sufferers may blame themselves and constantly relive the traumatic event. They may wonder how they could have prevented it, and will constantly live in shame or guilt as they blame themselves for the trauma.

These symptoms need to last more than a month and need to demonstrate an inability to control the symptoms. Mayo Clinic suggests you can define four categories of PTSD:

- Intrusive memories: unwanted or recurrent memories, even flashbacks or dreams of a traumatic event

- Avoidance: trying to avoid thinking or talking about the fearful event or avoid people or places associated with the trauma

- Negative changes in thinking or mood: being numb, negative, or disinterested in personal relationships

- Changes in emotional reactions: excessive arousal symptoms including frequent irritability, anger, guilt, shame, or even suicidal thoughts.

People at particular risk for developing PTSD are those who have suffered trauma for a prolonged period of time, such as prisoners of war or even childhood abuse victims. First responders may also be particularly prone to PTSD. Other major mental health disorder sufferers, like those with depression or GAD, are at risk, as are people without good support systems, with a genetically linked relative, or with a family history of PTSD and depression.

The diagnosis of PTSD is based on thorough mental and physical health exams. Again, you will hear use of DSM-5 criteria. These include having experienced or witnessed a traumatic event, had close association with people who did, or repeated exposure to the graphic details of a traumatic event. Having met one of those categories, then the patient must show signs or symptoms after the traumatic event of:

- Reliving the experience
- Having upsetting dreams or daytime flashbacks
- When reminded or the event, experiencing ongoing or intense emotional distress and symptoms

Additionally, if after one month of the traumatic event, you:

- Avoid similar circumstances
- Forget important parts of the trauma
- Have a negative world perspective or self-view
- Lose interest in people or activities
- Feel constantly numb, irritable, or angry
- Engage in dangerous or self-destructive behavior
- Are easily startled
- Suffer trouble sleeping or concentrating

Treatment includes:

- Psychotherapy
- Exposure therapy, which means using virtual reality programs that safely reenter the experienced trauma
- Eye movements desensitization and reprocessing (EMDR), which uses guided eye movement to help process how you react to trauma
- Medications: antidepressants, anti-anxiety meds, and also Prazosin, which is a medication that helps with anxiety or recurrent nightmares

Generally good self-care, following of your treatment plan, avoiding of self-medication, and finding PTSD support groups are very helpful. This seems to be particularly beneficial for veterans and first responders.

Further reading on symptoms of PTSD can be found online at:

www.activebeat.com

www.lifescript.com

www.mayoclinic.org

OBSESSIVE-COMPULSIVE DISORDER
(DSM-5 Category: Obsessive-Compulsive and Related Disorders)

There are many disorders listed under Obsessive-Compulsive and Related Disorders in the DSM-5. They include:

- Obsessive-compulsive disorder

- Body dysmorphic disorder

- Hoarding disorder

- Trichotillomania (hair-pulling disorder)

- Excoriation (skin-picking) disorder

- Substance/medication-induced

- Obsessive-compulsive and related disorder

- Obsessive-compulsive and related disorder due to another medical condition

- Other specified obsessive-compulsive and related disorder

- Unspecified obsessive-compulsive and related disorder

Obsessive-compulsive disorder (OCD) is extremely common and tends to be long-lasting in which a person has unreasonable, recurrent, and uncontrollable fears and thoughts (obsessions) and repetitive behaviors (compulsions). One can also have only obsessions, or only compulsions, but still have OCD.

The OCD sufferer feels driven to perform repetitive behaviors in an effort to diminish their stressful feelings. These fears seem to organize around a specific fear such as getting germs, leading to repetitive hand washing to the point of creating chapping or sores on the hands. The behavior becomes ritualistic and enters a vicious cycle of fear and behavior.

Some common obsessions include the aforementioned fear of germs; forbidden thoughts of sex, religion, or harm; aggressive self-destructive thoughts or harmful acts toward others; thoughts of yelling out obscenities; or arranging things in a symmetrical or perfect order.

Compulsions, the repetitive behaviors, are responses to obsessive thoughts, and common ones include excessive cleaning or hand washing, placing and organizing things in a particular and precise way, repeated checking of things like whether the door is locked or the light is left on, demanding reassurances, and compulsive counting aloud or silently.

Now lots of us check things twice. However, OCD patients spend at least one hour each day on these thoughts and behaviors, disrupting their daily life by excessive attention to these thoughts or behaviors. They are unable to control their thoughts and behaviors even when they recognize them as excessive.

Occasionally a person with OCD also develops a tic. Motor tics are sudden, brief, repetitive jerks or rapid movements of the face or eye, shoulder shrugging, or head movements. They may also develop vocal tics like sniffing, grunting, or throat-clearing.

People with OCD tend to try to self-control or self-medicate with drugs or alcohol. But it is not uncommon for parents, teacher, or colleagues to first point out the excessive and repetitive behavior, as the sufferer may not actually realize what he or she is doing.

It is not known what causes OCD; however, at least two causes seem probable:

1. Biology: changes in the body's own natural chemistry, brain function, or even a genetic component

2. Environment: factors triggering OCD such as infection

Risk factors for OCD include:

- Family history

- Stressful life events: dealing with stressful events by repetitive activity

The primary concern is that these thoughts and behaviors interrupt normal work or school, relationships, and also connect to other anxiety issues like depression, anorexia or bulimia, alcohol, marijuana, or other drug abuse, and physical distress like chapped hands from washing.

To diagnose OCD requires a thorough physical exam and lab tests to rule out other medical conditions, and then a complete psychological testing to meet DSM-5 criteria, which include:

- Obsessions, compulsions, or both

- Realizing or not realizing that your thoughts and behaviors are excessive

- Obsessions and compulsions being significantly time consuming and disruptive of your life

The treatment for OCD may not always completely eliminate these thoughts and behaviors, but should certainly reduce symptoms. Treatments include:

- Psychotherapy: Exposure and response prevention (ERP). You are gradually exposed to the fear (say, dirt) and then you learn healthy ways to cope with your anxiety. Here, family, group, or individual sessions may help.

- Medications: Antidepressants can be used in single or combination therapy, but it is absolutely critical not to stop medications without a physician's supervision. The therapist should try to use the lowest possible effective dosage. All of these medications have potentially significant side effects, and some suicidal thoughts or behaviors may occur especially in people below 25. If this occurs, a physician should be consulted immediately. There also can be troubling drug-drug interactions.

- Family support groups are very useful.

Finally, there are many new trials being conducted by the National Institute of Mental Health (NIMH) using newer medications, combination therapy, and even deep brain stimulation (DBS). You might wish to contact the NIMH at NIMH Clinical Trials—Participants (www.nimh.nih.gov/health/trials/index.shtml).

Further reading on this topic may be found by searching online at:

www.nimh.nih.gov

www.mayoclinic.org

www.helpguide.org

DEPRESSION
(DSM-5 Category: Depressive Disorders)

Although not considered an anxiety disorder, one of the most common mental illnesses in our culture is depression. People suffering from depression do experience significant anxiety. Some estimates suggest close to 40% of Americans have episodes of significant depression in their lifetimes. Therefore I believe at least a limited discussion of depressive disorders will be of benefit.

DSM-5 lists the following depressive disorders:

- Disruptive mood dysregulation disorder
- Major depressive disorder, single, and recurrent episodes
- Persistent depressive disorder (dysthymia)
- Premenstrual dysphoric disorder
- Substance/medication-induced depressive disorder
- Depressive disorder due to another medical condition
- Other specified depressive disorder
- Unspecified depressive disorder

I will focus on what is commonly known as clinical depression or major depressive disorder. The symptoms affect how you think, feel, and act in daily situations, and have significant impact on your sleep, eating, and functioning in the workplace.

The National Institutes of Mental Health and the DSM-5 break this disorder down into several major categories:

- Persistent depressive disorder: This is also called dysthymia, and it consists of a depressed mood that lasts for at least two years. Sufferers may have severe depression, interrupted by periods of lesser depression, but all in all lasting for at least two years.

- Perinatal depression: This is more serious than just the "baby blues" in which anxiety and depression last for about two weeks postpartum. The episodes of depression are severe and can occur during or after delivery and typically are characterized by severe sadness, anxiety, and complete exhaustion, making it impossible for these new mothers to care for themselves or their babies.

- Psychotic depression: This is characterized by severe depression accompanied by psychosis, such as belief delusions or auditory and/or visual hallucinations. The delusions have a depressive tone or theme such as delusions of guilt, poverty, or illness.

- Seasonal affective disorder: Generally this depression occurs during the winter months and eases in the spring and summer. The winter depression is accompanied by isolation and withdrawal, increased sleep, weight gain, and seems to occur year after year.

- Bipolar disorder: I am including a mention of this disorder here because someone with bipolar disorder has episodes of extremely low or dark moods that would meet the criteria of a major depression. However, in contrast, persons with bipolar disorder also have episodes of mania or extremely high mood in which they can be extremely euphoric or even irritable. However, I will also address bipolar disorder as its own entity, as it is of major interest in our society.

- There are additional depressive disorders in children and adolescents that we label as disruptive mood dysregulation disorder, and also premenstrual dysphoric disorder in women.

Here are a few of the more common signs or symptoms occurring in people suffering from depression. The doctor will make this diagnosis if these circumstances persist most of the day, nearly every day, or for at least two weeks.

- Persistent anxiety, sadness, or empty feeling

- Feelings of hopelessness or pessimism

- Irritability

- Feelings of helplessness, worthlessness, or guilt

- Loss of interest in activities, work, or hobbies that would normally bring pleasure

- Fatigue or loss of energy

- Trouble in making decisions, difficulty in concentrating, or difficulty in remembering

- Sleep disturbances: difficulty falling asleep, early morning awakening, or even repeated oversleeping

- Changes in appetite or weight

- Thoughts of death, suicide, or suicide attempts

- Digestive disorders, pains, headaches, muscle cramps without a clear physical cause and that don't easily go away with treatment

Not everyone with depression will experience all these symptoms. In fact, those who show just a few or minimal intensity of symptoms may have a somewhat hidden depression, making it very difficult to diagnose. It is important to describe all your symptoms or signs to your attending physician or therapist, even if you don't consider it significant. The therapist needs to assess your mental and emotional condition based on the total picture.

Most researchers feel that depression comes about through a variety of factors including genetics (often runs in families), biological features (accompanying other illnesses), environmental factors, and psychological stressors. Certainly major life crises can lead to full-blown depression.

It can come about at any age but often displays itself in adulthood. In children or teenagers, it may present with irritability rather than low mood.

Commonly, when we see children with "anxiety" in their childhood, they may develop depression as an adult.

Very frequently, we see depression accompanying illnesses like diabetes, Parkinson's, heart disease, or cancer, and occasionally the drugs used to treat these other illnesses may precipitate or worsen depression.

Treatment

Fortunately, depression is treatable, even in its most severe forms, and the earlier diagnosis and treatment are begun, the greater chance for successful outcomes.

Generally, depression is approached with multiple therapeutic arms: psychotherapy (guided talk therapy), medications, and good general healthcare are all helpful. If these treatments do not reduce symptoms, electroconvulsive therapy (ECT) and other brain stimulation therapies can be offered.

Psychotherapy

Psychotherapy, sometimes called "talk therapy" or counseling, can be very helpful for depression. Cognitive-behavioral therapy (CBT), interpersonal therapy (IPT), and problem-solving therapy can be especially effective. Visit the National Institutes of Mental Health website and search for the publication for "Depression: What You Need to Know" for more information.

While far from complete, I have listed several strong resources here to at least begin your journey toward effective psychotherapy care:

- Catholic Therapist: www.CatholicTherapists.com. This is a national referral source for counselors who share values consistent with the Catholic faith.

- The Pastoral Solutions Institute: www.CatholicCounselors.com. All counselors are licensed therapists with additional training in Catholic theology and spirituality.

- American Association of Pastoral Counselors (AAPC): www.aapc.org. The mission of the AAPC is to bring healing, hope, and wholeness to individuals, families, and communities by expanding and equipping spiritually grounded and psychologically informed care, counseling, and psychotherapy.

- National Christian Counselors Association (NCCA): www.ncca.org. Trains, certifies, and licenses Christian counselors, provides testing, and includes physicians, attorneys, and educators in mental health disorders.

- American Association of Christian Counselors (AACC): www.aacc.net. Includes 50,000 professional counselors, marriage and family therapists, social workers, psychiatrists, psychologists, and pastors.

Further reading

- The Food and Drug Administration addresses the safety and description of antidepressant medications. Visit www.fda.gov and search for a specific drug of concern.

- Search for "brain stimulation therapies" at www.nimh.nih.gov. See also:

  » *The World Journal of Biological Psychiatry (WFSBP)*, 2010;11:2-18, guidelines on brain stimulation treatments

  » *Motivation, Emotion, Feeding, Drinking, Sexual Behavior,* NeuroReport 6, 1853-1856 (1995) on rTMS

  » www.ncbi.nlm.nih.gov and related articles, Bergfeld, IO, et al, *Deep Brain Stimulation of the Ventral Anterior Limb of the*

Internal Capsule for Treatment-Resistant Depression, Bergfeld, IO, et al, JAMA Psychiatry, May 1;73(50):456-464

- Drs. David Ludwig and Mary Jacob, *Christian Concepts for Care,* Concordia Publishing House, St. Louis, 2015

More medical information can be received from consultation with your physician. Also explore the Mayo Clinic website (www.mayoclinic.org) for diseases and conditions, mental illnesses, and psychosis. See also the National Institutes of Mental Health to search for schizophrenia, bipolar, depression, etc.

Medications

Antidepressants are the main category of medical therapy. These medications alter the way your brain uses certain chemicals that control stress or your mood. It may take one or a combination of drugs to achieve symptom relief. If you have a family history of depression, it appears that some drugs are helpful to each member in the family. An important feature of medications is to understand that it takes two to four weeks for these drugs to act, so you cannot make snap judgments as to their success or failure. Most importantly, do not stop taking medications without your physician's supervision. Often there is a temptation to stop taking the medications as soon as one starts feeling better, merely to discover that the depression quickly returns. Generally, depression medical therapy will require six to 12 months of continuous therapy, after which you and your physician may slowly and safely decrease your dosage. Abrupt withdrawal of medications can produce severe withdrawal symptoms.

One significant note regarding the use of antidepressants in children or adolescents: under age 25, people may experience an increase in suicidal thoughts or behavior when taking antidepressants, especially in the first few weeks of therapy or after a dosage change. Everyone taking antidepressants, whether adult or child, must be monitored closely.

Although generally safe to take during pregnancy or nursing, a full discussion should be held with your doctor about side effects and risk/benefits, even if you are considering getting pregnant in the near future. For further information on all these medications, you can visit www.fda.gov and explore specific medications and side effects.

Let me offer a final word about home remedies or herb supplements. There has been much interest in St. John's wort. There is no reputable scientific evidence at present for the efficacy or safety of this herbal supplement at present. Talk to your doctor. The same goes for omega-3 fatty acids and SAMe or S-adenosylmethionine. Please consult your physician and visit the National Center for Complementary and Integrative Health.

Brain stimulation therapy

If psychotherapy and medications do not reduce symptoms of depression, Electroconvulsive therapy (ECT) may be worth pursuing. ECT has been shown to provide relief in people who have failed other modalities. It can be used in situations where rapid relief is sought or medications cannot be used safely. It can be given in an outpatient setting and is generally given over a period of two to four weeks and perhaps three sessions per week.

There can be significant side effects from ECT, including persistent memory loss or confusion. Generally, these resolve rather quickly but can persist for months. The newer anesthetic medications and procedures have made this therapy much safer and more tolerable.

There are also newer brain stimulation therapies including repetitive transcranial magnetic stimulations (rTMS) and vagus nerve stimulation (VNS). Please visit the NIMH Brain Stimulation Therapies webpage for more information.

Additional therapy for depression

As we have mentioned with all these disorders, there are many general health strategies that will assist in your recovery from mental disorders:

- Exercise and be active

- Eat nutritionally: lots of vegetables, fruits, and whole grains

- Set realistic goals

- Spend time with family and friends and your faith community

- Expect gradual improvement rather than sudden change

- Try to avoid major life decisions like getting married, pregnant, divorced, or accepting major job change until you feel better and you are thinking more clearly

- Seek group therapy and support

- Continue to educate yourself about your condition

Further reading

- National Institute of Mental Health: Depression: What You Need to Know at www.nimh.nih.gov

- Food and Drug Administration: Safety and description of antidepressant medications: www.fda.gov

- Brain Stimulation Therapies: Search online at www.nimh.nih.gov or see *The World Journal of Biological Psychiatry (WFSBP)*, 2010;11:2-18, guidelines on brain stimulation treatments; *Motivation, Emotion, Feeding, Drinking, Sexual Behavior*, NeuroReport 6, 1853-1856 (1995) *on* rTMS; www.ncbi.nlm.nih.gov and related articles, Bergfeld, IO, et al, "Deep Brain Stimulation of the Ventral Anterior Limb of the Internal Capsule for Treatment-Resistant Depression," Bergfeld, IO, et al, *JAMA Psychiatry*, May 1; 73(50):456-464.

- Drs. David Ludwig's and Mary Jacob's book, *Christian Concepts for Care*, Concordia Publishing House, St. Louis, 2015.

More medical information can be received from consultation with your physician or also from exploring the Mayo Clinic website. (See www.mayoclinic.org under diseases and conditions, mental illnesses, psychosis, etc. You may also visit the National Institutes of Mental Health website www.nimh.nih.gov under schizophrenia, bipolar, depression, etc.).

BIPOLAR DISORDER

Bipolar disorder is discussed apart from depressive disorders because of its characteristics and difficulty in treatment, and because of its prominence in contemporary cultural conversation and mental health education. Unfortunately, since this disorder appears to have increasing public awareness and in a sense has been "popularized," there is a great risk that skewed, false, or biased information is in the public media. For example, it is a misconception that all people with bipolar disorder can become violent. Sadly, so too can people with heart disease, diabetes, and cancer. Some people with bipolar disorder can become aggressive and demonstrate violence, but that does not imply that by any means should all people with bipolar disorder be feared.

More than half of people who develop bipolar disorder do so before age 25. The condition affects nearly six million adults in the U.S., nearly 5.7% of the adult population.

Bipolar disorder used to be called manic depression. It is characterized by extreme mood swings that swing from the lows of depression to the emotional highs, also called mania or hypomania (see definitions below). In the depressive phase people feel sad, hopeless, and lose pleasure and interest in activities. However, the depression may give way to a euphoric, energetic phase. These mood phases may swing several times per week or perhaps only two or three times per year.

Bipolar disorder is a chronic illness but is certainly treatable, with many sufferers achieving good control through psychotherapy and carefully following a treatment plan. If on medications as a part of that plan, working closely with a mental health professional is imperative to assure avoiding rapidly stopping medications or self-medicating with other mood-altering substances.

It is most important to understand and diagnose bipolar disorder accurately because there are several types of this disorder. For each form of bipolar disorder there are appropriate forms of treatment. However, some medications used commonly can have adverse effects if not used in the appropriate diagnosis. There are even person-to-person differences in symptoms and signs among people with exactly the same diagnostic type of bipolar disorder.

DSM-5, published by the American Psychiatric Association, lists the following types of bipolar and related disorders:

Bipolar I disorder: You have to have demonstrated at least one manic episode. That episode can be preceded by an episode of depression or hypomania. The manic episode can substantially impair your living, might require that you be hospitalized, or might lead you to lose touch with reality, which is called *psychosis*. There is a list of nine symptoms below listed under depressive episodes; you must demonstrate five of the nine symptoms during the same two-week period to be diagnosed as a depressive episode.

Bipolar II disorder: You demonstrate at least one major depressive episode lasting at least two weeks, and you have experienced one hypomanic episode for at least four days, but you have never had a manic episode. Again, the major depressive phase or the unpredictable changes in your mood and behavior substantially disrupt your life. It is important to note that Bipolar II disorder is not merely a milder form of Bipolar I disorder but a separate illness. Bipolar I disorder's manic episodes can be severe and dangerous, but people with Bipolar II disorder can have very prolonged depressive episodes as well.

Cyclothymic disorder: You've experienced at least two years, or one year as a child or teenager, with numerous episodes of hypomanic symptoms and periods of depressive symptoms, but neither low or high moods are severe in nature. During that two-year period your symptoms are happening at least half the time and never leave you for more than two months. Symptoms significantly disrupt your life.

Other types: The "other types" include bipolar symptoms and signs which are actually brought about by another medical condition like multiple sclerosis, Cushing's disease (low adrenal secretion), or strokes. Additionally, substance abuse and medicine can induce bipolar symptoms.

It will be helpful to understand the meaning of these various terms: manic and hypomanic.

Manic episode: A well-defined period of abnormality with persistent elevated, expansive, or irritable mood that lasts at least one week. If you require hospitalization, that time frame can be counted even if less than one week. That manic episode includes persistently increased goal-directed activity or energy. To be considered manic, the mood episodes must:

Be severe enough to require hospitalization, demonstrate a break with reality, threaten harm to yourself or others, or cause substantial difficulty at work, school, or in social settings. The symptoms can't be related to substance abuse of drugs or alcohol, medication, or medical conditions.

Hypomanic episode: A well-defined period of abnormal and persistently elevated, expansive, or irritable mood that goes on for at least four days. Hypomanic episodes demonstrate:

- A distinct, uncharacteristic change in mood or function that even other people notice

- No evidence of significant trouble at work, school, or in social situations, and doesn't require hospitalization, and doesn't cause psychosis

- Symptoms as a result of alcohol or drugs, medications, or other medical conditions

Whether a manic or hypomanic episode, at least three or more of the following symptoms must be present and be substantially different from your usual behavior:

- Inflated self-esteem or grandiosity; you feel self-assured, confident, and incapable of being wrong

- Unusual talkativeness; more rapid or open speech

- Racing thoughts or a flight of ideas; you can't slow down your thoughts

- Easy distractibility

- Decreased need for sleep; sleeping less but not feeling bothered by the decrease; you feel rejuvenated after only two or three hours of rest

- Agitation or increased goal-directed activity

- Behaving unusually and doing things that have high negative consequences, such as buying sprees, foolish business adventures, or sexual indiscretions

Major depressive episodes, as defined by DSM-5 criteria, are characterized by five or more symptoms listed below occurring over a two-week period that demonstrates a change from your usual moods. These can be self-reported or reported by others.

- Feeling sad, empty, hopeless, tearful, or irritable most of the day, nearly every day

- Weight loss or weight gain, altered appetite nearly every day when you are not trying to diet

- Reduced interest in life, feeling no joy or pleasure every day or throughout the day

- Insomnia (too little sleep) or hypersomnia (too much sleep) nearly every day as compared to your previous baseline state, including trouble falling asleep, staying asleep, or early morning awakening

- Restlessness or very slowed behavior noticeable to others; this can also be seen as very slow or very sped-up speech

- Fatigue or energy loss every day

- Feelings of worthlessness or excessive guilt (feeling bad about what you have done) nearly every day; thinking that you do not matter or that people wouldn't care whether you're dead or alive; may also involve shame (feeling bad about who you are)

- Inability to concentrate or being indecisive every day

- Recurrent thoughts of suicide or death, suicide planning, or attempts

These depressive symptoms must be severe enough to disrupt day-to-day activities or relationships. They cannot be caused by drugs or other medical conditions and should not be caused by grieving like after the death of a loved one.

A few additional symptoms and signs can be seen in bipolar disorder including catatonia (not reacting to your environment or holding your body in an unusual position), seasonal mood changes, melancholia (loss of pleasure even when good things happen), psychosis (loss of reality, hallucinations or delusions that are false but strongly held beliefs), and finally, onset of symptoms during pregnancy or within four weeks after delivery.

Children and teenagers may demonstrate distinct manic, hypomanic, and depressive episodes but may return to their usual behavior between episodes. Moods can shift rapidly during acute episodes. This can be a difficult diagnosis in young people.

Bipolar disorder does not get better on its own. If you recognize these symptoms in yourself or others, see a doctor or mental health provider. People with bipolar disorder often don't recognize how much the illness is disrupting their lives or the lives of their family. Some people with bipolar disorder enjoy the euphoria and high energy as they seem to get more done. But the euphoria is always followed by crashes in their mood and depression and may even leaves them with financial, legal, or social trouble.

It is good to recognize when you might need emergency assistance. If you have suicidal thoughts or behavior, please call 911 or an emergency operator immediately. You may also try to contact a loved one or friend, get ahold of your pastor or someone in your faith community, or call a suicide hotline such as the National Suicide Prevention Lifeline (800-273-8255). If you are a veteran, call that same number and press 1 to reach someone with focused interest in the care of veterans. If this is a loved one you are concerned about, make sure to keep someone with the suicidal person while you obtain help if you can.

Causes of bipolar disorder

The exact cause(s) of bipolar disorder is unknown but contributing components can include physical changes in the brain, imbalances in neurotransmitters (chemicals) in the brain, or even inherited traits. Bipolar disorder does seem to occur frequently in some families.

Additionally, bipolar disorder seems to be triggered by periods of high stress, drug or alcohol abuse, traumatic experiences, or deaths of loved ones.

Unfortunately, if you have bipolar disorder, you may simultaneously have a variety of the anxiety disorders we have discussed earlier such as GAD, PTSD, ADHD (attention-deficit/hyperactivity disorder), or addiction and substance abuse.

Make lists to help your healthcare provider make a proper diagnosis.

- List key symptoms and how long they have been occurring.

- Assemble key personal information, major stresses, and life changes.

- Document all medication, even vitamins and supplements.

- Gather a list of questions you want to ask.

- Have a family member or friend to go with you to help you listen and ask questions.

Your mental health or medical care provider will probably request the following procedures:

- Thorough physical exam including blood work

- A psychological evaluation including talking with you about your

- thoughts, feelings, or behavior. You might fill out a mental health questionnaire, and the therapist might want to ask family and friends their observations of your behavior or moods.

- Mood charting that includes a daily diary of your moods, thoughts, sleep, or eating patterns, all of which can help to find the right treatment for you

Treatment of bipolar disorder

The team leader in the treatment of bipolar disorder will be a psychiatrist, which is a medical doctor specializing in mental health and disease. Your team may also include a psychologist, social worker, psychiatric nurse, and possibly even a nutritionist.

Your treatment will have several parts to it, including:

- Initial therapy: Medication will be prescribed to help regulate your moods and will be adjusted carefully to give the best long-term treatment. We will discuss the types of medications momentarily.

- Continued therapy: Bipolar treatment is life-long, even when you are feeling improved. Maintenance medications are essential and one of the most difficult issues is for bipolar patients to understand

and accomplish staying on medications. Stopping medication presents a very high risk of developing a relapse of symptoms or even intense mania or depression.

- Support and counseling programs on an outpatient basis are imperative.

- If you also have substance abuse or alcohol issues, you must also seek treatment for these disorders as well as bipolar disorder.

- Hospitalization may be necessary if you are suicidal or showing dangerous behavior, or if you feel detached from reality. This can save your life and keep you calm and stable.

Medications for bipolar disorder

- Mood stabilizers: These are useful for Bipolar I or II and helpful to control manic or hypomanic episodes. These include lithium, valproic acid (Depakene), divalproex sodium (Depakote), carbamazepine (Tegretol, Equetro), and lamotrigine (Lamictal).

- Antipsychotics: If your symptoms of depression or mania persist despite treatment with other meds, you may be prescribed antipsychotic medications like olanzapine (Zyprexa), risperidone (Risperdal), or quetiapine (Seroquel), as well as others.

- Antidepressants: If depression is difficult to control, your doctor may prescribe an antidepressant. Note that on occasion an antidepressant can trigger a manic episode, so it may often be prescribed along with a mood stabilizer or antipsychotic.

- Antidepressant-antipsychotic: The medication Symbyax combines an antidepressant with an antipsychotic, so it combines the effect of an antidepressant and mood stabilizer. It is approved by the Food and Drug Administration to treat Bipolar I Disorder.

- Anti-anxiety medications: Benzodiazepines, used to treat anxiety, can help relieve anxiety or assist in sleep on a short-term basis. Common examples include Valium, Xanax, Klonopin, Ativan, Halcion, Restoril, and Tranxene.

With the use of multiple medications, side effects and adverse drug effects or interactions are a significant threat to health. Talk to your mental health professional whenever new signs or symptoms develop. Do not self-medicate! Do not stop or start medication on your own without consultation with your doctor. You will feel improved when you find the right medications and doses and your body adjusts to these medications. Please stay with your therapist; it may take trial and error to get the medications right. Be patient and give it time to get the full benefits of the medications. Your doctor will normally try to change just one medication at a time and then observe your response before changing medications or altering the dose.

Since some medications used to treat bipolar disorder can cause birth defects, if you are of childbearing age, immediately discuss this issue with your doctor so you can explore birth control options. Examine treatment options if you become pregnant, and clarify if your medications can be passed through breast milk if you choose to breastfeed your baby.

Psychotherapy

Psychotherapy, or guided talk therapy, remains a major part of your treatment plan for all bipolar disorders. It can be provided individually to you, with your family in attendance, or even in a group of people suffering the same illness. Here are a few of the different types of psychotherapy your doctor may suggest:

- Cognitive behavioral therapy: The core of this therapy is to replace negative and unhealthy beliefs and behaviors with healthy, positive ones. Your therapist will help you determine what seems to trigger your manic, hypomanic, or depressive episodes. They can give you skills and strategies to manage your stress and help you cope with situations that might upset you.

- Psychoeducation: It is important for you and your family to understand your bipolar illness and for all of you to recognize the warning signs of mood swings.

- Interpersonal and social rhythm therapy (IPSRT): This therapy helps you stabilize the daily patterns of sleep, eating, exercise, and times you are awake. If you can get into a more consistent rhythm of life, you can better manage your moods.

- Other therapies: This might include diet or supplement therapy, yoga, meditation, and other forms worth discussing with your therapist.

Additional treatment options

Occasionally other types of treatment might be helpful to stabilize your bipolar disorder:

- Electroconvulsive therapy (ECT): Electrical currents are passed through your brain while you are sedated and closely monitored. It appears that the currents affect the levels of brain chemicals (neurotransmitters) and can even bring rapid or immediate relief to severe depressive episodes when other therapies don't work. Some people experience memory loss and headaches that are generally temporary and limited. Most often ECT is limited to people who can't take antidepressants, are at high risk of suicide, or aren't improving on medications and psychotherapy. Occasionally it might be used during pregnancy when you can't take other medications.

- Transcranial magnetic stimulation (TMS): This is another option for people who don't respond well to antidepressants. With this treatment you are placed in a reclining position in a chair, and magnetic coils are placed on your scalp. These coils send very brief magnetic pulses to stimulate nerve cells in the brain that seem to be involved in depression and regulation of mood. This typically involves five treatments per week for up to six weeks.

Treatment of bipolar disorder in children and teenagers

Many aspects of treatment will be adjusted in younger sufferers of bipolar disorder to help control symptoms and avoid disruptive side effects:

- Medications: Generally, the same types of medications are given to children and teenagers with bipolar disorder. Unfortunately, the safety and effectiveness has only been studied in adults, so decisions on therapy are made on a case-by-case basis.

- Psychotherapy: This is always required and helpful to children and teenagers and can help them develop appropriate coping skills. It can also assist in helping learning challenges and styles, helping with social relationships with friends and family, and improving communication. It can also help with substance abuse, which tends to be more common with older children who are bipolar.

- Family and school support: Getting the entire school and home team involved in bipolar care can make an immense difference in the success and stability of care of bipolar disorder in children.

Lifestyle changes

Finally, there are many lifestyle changes that can stop mood swings and challenging behavior in bipolar disorder:

- Stop substance abuse, illegal drugs, and alcohol. This is a major difficulty with bipolar disorder and will often require outside help to quit as it is so difficult to do on your own.

- Try to avoid unhealthy relationships. Try to surround yourself with positive people who don't encourage unhealthy or risky behavior.

- Exercise and stay active. Your mood is much improved when you get regular, moderate exercise. It helps relieve stress, improves sleep, and helps your body and emotions stay steady. Always check with your doctor to make sure you can exercise safely. If you are taking lithium, check with your doctor to make sure the exercise doesn't interfere with lithium levels or effectiveness.

- Get adequate sleep. Don't be a night owl. Getting enough sleep, generally about eight hours per night, is critically important in managing your mood. If this remains an issue, talk with your therapist for suggestions.

- Consider alternate or complementary therapies. Unfortunately there is not adequate study at this point to make strong recommendations, but here are a few optional therapies to discuss with your doctor:

  » Consider trying Omega-3 fatty acids. Fish oils or omega-3s seem to be helpful as a supplement for bipolar disorder in some people.

  » Consider trying magnesium. There are a few studies showing some benefit in terms of lessening manic episodes; more study is needed.

  » There might be some benefit to St. John's wort. This is used in some cultures to help depression; however, this herb may actually interact with some antidepressant medications, and it has even been reported to trigger mania in some people.

  » Many ancient and modern cultures use acupuncture. The Chinese treat depression with this form of sticking thin needles into the skin. It appears safe, although its full efficacy is unknown.

» Consider trying herbs. Again, the Chinese have been using a combination of herbs to treat a variety of mental disorders; the efficacy is unknown.

» Some therapists suggest S-adenosyl-L-methionine (SAMe). This amino acid supplement has been used in depression. The effectiveness is unknown and there have been reports of SAMe triggering manic episodes.

Regarding all of these supplements, never stop taking your prescribed medications from your therapists without their full knowledge and consent. Please be honest with them, letting them know what you are taking. Continue to be highly cautious; understand and study all risks and benefits, and be knowledgeable about your health and interactions with other medications.

Finally, be educated about your disorder. Keep your long- and short-term goals in mind. Don't be afraid to have strong outside and family support groups. Find healthy ways to channel and release excess energy and learn ways to handle and diminish stress, like exercise, tai chi, yoga, meditation, prayer, or even massage therapy.

Above all, pay attention to warning signs that might mean an attack is coming soon. Call your therapist, and involve your family and friends in helping you identify warning signs.

Stay away from illicit drugs and alcohol, all of which actually worsen your symptoms and can trigger a relapse. Take your medications exactly as the therapist has prescribed them. *Don't* stop taking them, even if you think you are feeling better; call your doctor to discuss any changes. Remember to talk to your therapist if you are considering taking alternative or complementary supplements, and even when you are prescribed any medications from another physician, just to make sure the new medications don't interact adversely with your bipolar medications.

Additional information

- Search for "bipolar disorder" at www.mayoclinic.org

- Search for "depression" at the National Institute of Mental Health at www.nimh.nih.gov

- Search for "bipolar disorder in children and adolescents" at the National Institute of Mental Health at www.nimh.nih.gov

- Ravindran AV, et al., "Complementary and Alternative Therapies as Add-ons to Pharmacotherapy for Mood and Anxiety Disorders: a Systematic Review," *Journal of Affective Disorders.* 2013; 150:707

- Frye MA. Clinical practice. Bipolar disorder—A Focus on Depression," *New England Journal of Medicine.* 2011:364:51

PAINTER/POINTER COMMUNICATION TYPOGRAPHY SCALE

REV. DR. DAVID LUDWIG

Circle the number that shows the degree to which one of the two descriptions fits your personality (3 is neutral).

1. When upset, can focus on something else and forget about things.   1 2 3 4 5   When upset, things stay stirred up inside and cannot easily be pushed aside.

2.* When upset, needs to be with others to talk over things.   5 4 3 2 1   When upset, needs space to be alone and let things settle down.

3.* Is comfortable feeling and expressing emotion   5 4 3 2 1   Feeling and expressing emotion is unsettling.

4. Is usually not tuned in to subtle emotional cues.   1 2 3 4 5   Is sensitive to subtle cues from others.

5. Can focus on one thing and be oblivious of other things going on.   1 2 3 4 5   When trying to concentrate on one thing, is also aware of other things going on.

6.* Can be doing many things at once—is good at shifting back and forth.   5 4 3 2 1   Is best at doing only one thing at a time—difficult to shift back and forth.

7. Tends to minimize the emotional importance of a situation (no big deal).   1 2 3 4 5   Tends to overstate the emotional importance for effect—to get through.

8. Will get right to the point; will summarize and give generalizations.

1 2 3 4 5

Will paint a picture—will give different details as they come to mind.

9.* Feels best when can be expressive and be the center of attention.

5 4 3 2 1

Is a good listener and feels best when the other person is in a good mood.

10. The first thing said is normally the point.

1 2 3 4 5

The first thing said is rarely the point.

11. When the other person is upset, will tend to withdraw.

1 2 3 4 5

When the other person is upset, will try to make contact.

12.* Will state feelings based on what is felt at the moment.

5 4 3 2 1

Will summarize feelings over time and state summary.

13.* Will tend to flash all possible scenarios so that will not be surprised.

5 4 3 2 1

Will tend to overlook what can go wrong so as to stay optimistic about things.

14.* Moods will fluctuate moment to moment.

5 4 3 2 1

Moods will usually stay fairly even.

15.* Will feel a definite emotional reaction; things seem black or white

5 4 3 2 1

Will tend to see different sides and be ambiguous as to how to react.

* indicated when the numbering is reversed, going in descending order from 5 to 1

Add the numbers up. If below 45, you have *pointer* tendencies. If above 45, you have *painter* tendencies.

Painter/Pointer Communication Typography Scale used with permission of Rev. Dr. David Ludwig.

WORD-SATURATED MEDITATIVE PRAYER

There are many Biblical texts helpful with various causes of fear. Before entering a discussion of meditative or Word-saturated prayer, here are just a few suggestions, although by no means complete, to consider for your meditation with connections to specific causes of fear and anxiety:

"For God did not give us a spirit of timidity [*fear*], but a spirit of power, of love, and of self-discipline." (2 Timothy 1:7) St. Paul is urging Timothy to stir up his spiritual gifts, to testify for Jesus, and to share with Paul in the sufferings of the act of spreading the Gospel of Christ. We may be ostracized for witnessing about Jesus, be fearful of new relationships, or new enterprises. We remember that it is Satan who was handing out the fear stimuli, not Jesus. Jesus' "perfect love drives out fear." (1 John 4:18)

In Hebrews 13:5 and Matthew 28:20 we hear that many people have fear surrounding loneliness. Rather, we need to trust and experience the fact that from our Baptism onward, we are not alone. Jesus tells us, "Never will I leave you; never will I forsake you." To which the Scripture assures us and we can "...say with confidence, 'The Lord is my helper; I will not be afraid. What can man do to me?'"

"The Lord is my light and my salvation—whom shall I fear? The Lord is the stronghold of my life—of whom shall I be afraid?" (Psalm 27:1) Whether it is cancer, or heart disease, or chronic neurological disorders, or mental illness, or natural calamities, or terrorism that call us to the darkened places in our lives, we know we have light and life in Jesus. In any threatening situation, we recall with the Psalmist, "God is our refuge and strength, an ever-present help in trouble. Therefore, I will not fear, though the earth gives way and the mountains fall into the heart of the sea...The Lord Almighty is with us; the God of Jacob is our fortress." (Psalm 46:1-11). Psalm 91, paraphrased in a wonderful spiritual hymn called "Eagle's

Wings" by Father Michael Joncas, is also applicable to the joys and stresses of life and death.

And one more reassurance from King David: "The Lord is my shepherd, I shall not want...Yea, though I walk through the valley of the shadow of death, I will fear no evil: For Thou art with me ...Surely goodness and mercy shall follow me all the days of my life, and I will dwell in the house of the Lord forever." (Psalm 23, KJV) If you have had any medical or emotional illness, suffered the loss of a loved one, or faced any separation from the people and purposes that you hold so closely, you will find comfort in David's psalm.

Biblically based preaching of the Word through the pastor's sermon or homily is another powerful conduit for bringing balm to our fearful illnesses. Commonly, the pastor begins his message by asking the Holy Spirit to be in the meditation of our hearts and minds as God's Word is shared with us. Hopefully, and most appropriately, the pastor's message is anchored in God's Word in the Bible. Although it is helpful to work other writings of literature into the message, the power of the pastor's reflections comes from sharing God's words and will for us from the Scriptures.

I would also suggest that praying God's Word in devotional time, meditatively, or in corporate worship is another essential way to *fear and love the Lord.* I want to bring you some comments on meditative prayer of God's holy Word that I think provide some practical invitations particularly in the setting of *anxiety.*

Being Present in Prayer: Word-Saturated Meditative Prayer

Have you ever found yourself in a conversation where you realized that you weren't *present,* where you were not listening to the other's communication with you? Have you experienced this as a pastor, chaplain, counselor, nurse, physician, or just as a friend? You know the situation: you're sitting at the bedside, or face-to-face across the table, but your mind and heart are far away. You are kidding yourself if you think those you are caring for are not picking up on your absence! Have you recognized your inattention during a conversation or during your time of prayer with your Creator, Redeemer, and Faith Builder?

We live in a multitasking society. There are constant threats to obstruct and disrupt our relationships and discourse with each other and with God. Most frequently, I would suggest, the threats of *noise* and *hurry* predominate in our culture and our time. I invite you to consider *pausing* physically, emotionally, and even spiritually before entering times of communication; this applies also to times of communication with God. I would ask you to consider entering these moments of conversation, even moments of prayer, by approaching them with quiet, solitude, stillness, and deeply and thoroughly filled, yes, *saturated in God's Word*.

Let's turn first to the disruptors of noise and hurry. I believe these two great threats to our communication are used by the devil, the world, and our own flesh to absent us from intentionally sitting at the feet of our Savior, God's Word. Noise and hurry seem to be prominent in times of anxiety and fear. These distractions are always present, especially as we work with the people God has placed in our care as pastors, chaplains, spiritual guides, nurses, physicians, or members in our personal family, faith family, and merely out in the world. Anxious noise and hurry accompany the threats and dangers in all of our lives.

Let us look at *noise*. Our environment is filled with sight and sound, but especially auditory stimulation. We are bombarded by radio, television, Internet, YouTube, and Pandora. We are constantly plugged in and often tuned out to the important conversations with those immediately around us. This external noise is amplified by our negative self-talk. Do you find yourself gently giving yourself a self-hug? Or do you more often greet yourself, or reflect on your behavior or choices with words like *idiot, stupid, dumbbell,* or other self-deprecating names? I would say we are usually the perfect setup for Satan to establish a base of operations to try to separate us from each other and from our Savior. Wouldn't it be healthier to find a corner of quiet, a cleft in the Rock of Ages, in which to hear God's voice?

And then there's *hurry*. Chief of sinners have I been in my life as a physician, husband, father, and friend. I love the quote of the 19th-century counselor and analytical psychiatrist Carl Jung, who said, "Hurry is not of the devil; it is the devil." Jung was probably paraphrasing St. Jerome from the fourth century, who said, "*Omnis festinatio ex parte diabolic est.*" ("All haste is of the devil.") We are constantly multitasking or distractedly single-tasking our way through life.

As opposed to noise and hurry, the Holy Scripture gives us several beautiful examples of a call to quiet ourselves and to slow down. In the Old Testament we remember the prophet Elijah. We recall Elijah as he is exhausted after being chased by Jezebel. (1 Kings 19:1-18) After destroying the prophets of Baal, God calls him to a time and a place of solitude, rest, restoration, and healing. How does the Creator come to Elijah? In a *whisper...*

When it is noisy we cannot hear a *whisper...*

From the New Testament, Jesus is coming to visit his family friends, Mary and Martha of Bethany. Martha is busying herself with preparations. She's clattering dishes and scurrying to cook and clean. Mary, her sister, is sitting at the feet of the Word, listening. Jesus honors Mary's choice. (Luke 10:38-42)

From Christ's lips at the Sermon on the Mount, we hear,

> "And when you pray, do not be like the hypocrites; for they love to pray standing in the synagogues...to be seen by men...they have received their reward in full. *But when you pray, go into your room, close the door and pray to your Father who is unseen...* for your Father knows what you need before you ask him. Then

this is how you should pray: 'Our Father in heaven...'" (Matthew 6:5-14, italics added)

Finally, from Luther's great Bible-based Christmas hymn, *Vom Himmel Hoch,* the verse:

"Ah, dearest Jesus, holy Child,

Make thee a bed, soft, undefiled,

Within my heart that it may be,

A quiet chamber kept for thee."

So in the settings of anxiety, noise, and hurry, might it be healthier to *pause* our conversations with things of the world in order to come to the Word of the Lord in quiet, unhurried prayer? Might it be better to remember, through God's Word, who is the Great Physician, the Almighty God, the maker and preserver of creation, to whom we are reconciled by Christ? Would it not set us on a steadier path of restoration of our health to have the Holy Spirit lead us to love, fear, and trust in God, to know by faith that God is listening to our prayer, and to follow God's will for all that afflicts us?

When we enter prayer by quieting, by settling and silencing our hearts as we hear the words of the Holy Scriptures, allowing ourselves the gift of solitude and being fully present, then the chamber of our heart is prepared to hear God's comfort, hope, and healing. His grace is always there. His grace is always present in Christ.

Let me share what I have found to be helpful to this practice of *Word-saturated meditative prayer* to provide a *pause point* in our journey, especially when challenged by fear and anxiety.

The Practice of Word-Saturated Meditative Prayer

I like to think of setting aside time to saturate our prayer life and centering ourselves in Christ, by praying the Word of God, speaking in God's language, aligning ourselves with God's will. This may be done with a quiet and unhurried approach to God's Word.

The practice of meditating on God's Word has a significant history within the Christian faith. I would, again, include Mary of Bethany sitting at the Lord's feet from the Scriptures as one example. Along the Emmaus journey of the Church, we have seen further models of meditative prayer: in Origen, the indisputable master of the Alexandrian school of theology, transferred to the Latin by St. Ambrose; Lectio Divina, established by St. Augustine from studying Ambrose; Martin Luther's Oratio, Meditatio, Tentatio, as well as his encouragement to pray the Psalter; and, furthermore, the Second Vatican Council's recommendation of the renewed value of Lectio Divina brought to a practical contemporary application through contemplative outreach under Father Thomas Keating, O.C.S.O., currently residing at St. Benedict's Trappist Monastery in Snowmass, Colorado.

All of these church leaders have called us back to mindfully spending time listening to and reflecting on what God self-reveals, and especially what God tells us about the saving and substitutionary sacrifice Jesus has done for us in his death and resurrection. These disciplines set our intention on the cross of Christ in quiet, focused, supplicating, receiving, and thankful postures before God's throne of grace and mercy.

Through our Grace Place Wellness Retreats (www.graceplacewellness. org) we offer Christ-centered meditation through a practice we call *Word-saturated meditative prayer*. Generally it follows the four-part, circular, prayer-pattern of Lectio Divina. Let me share that form of prayer with you in the hope that you might find it valuable in your spiritual walk with the Savior. In this meditative prayer practice we place Luther's concepts of Oratio, Meditatio, and Tentatio into a finite time frame for the purpose of praying "hours" of daily prayer (although that was not necessarily the specific intent of Luther's guidance to us).

Word-Saturated Meditation
QUIETING AND SLOWING DOWN

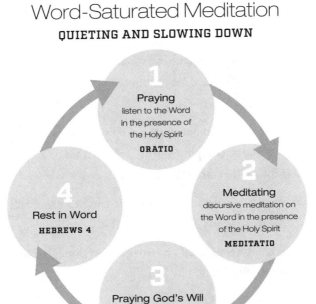

Choose Scripture text:

Choose a brief section of the Scriptures on which to meditate. Merely a few verses from any chapter will suffice. You may choose this randomly, by just opening the Bible, or you may follow a prescribed sequence from a devotional guide or a lectionary appropriate to the season.

Might I suggest one of these passages to consider for reflecting on *anxiety*?

"The Lord is my Shepherd, I shall not want..." (Psalm 23)

"The Lord takes pleasure in those who fear him, in those who hope in his steadfast love." (Psalm 147:11)

"Preserve me, O God, for in you I take refuge..." (Psalm 16:1-2, 5, 8-9, 11)

"To you, O Lord, I lift up my soul; in You I trust..." (Psalm 25:1-2, 6, 16-18, 20)

"The Lord is my light and my salvation; whom shall I fear?" (Psalm 27:1, 4-5, 7-8, 13-14) Examples of Jesus healing every disease. (Matthew 4:23-24)

"The Spirit helps us in our weakness...the Spirit intercedes for us with groaning too deep for words...If God is for us, who can be against us..." (Romans 8:26-32, 35-39)

"...Fear not for I am with you...I will strengthen you, I will help you..." (Isaiah 41:9b-10)

"...Who comforts us in all our troubles...so through Christ our comfort overflows..."

(2 Corinthians 1:3-5)

"Cast all your anxiety on him because he cares for you." (1 Peter 5:7)

Before entering the prayer, begin with:

Quieting: I invite you to begin by taking a few moments of quieting, breathing slowly and deeply. Try a five-count to breathe in, and a seven-count to breathe out. In doing this, your body quiets, your pulse and blood pressure reduce.

With a slowing and quieting of your body, you can proceed in the quieting of your mind. You may let go of the internal conversation that can often be so distracting, to begin meditating on the Word. Sometimes it is helpful to replace your own thoughts with a *breath prayer*, such as, "Lord (as you inhale), have mercy (as you exhale)." The use of a word or phrase like this helps to quiet both your mind and spirit, so that, like Mary at Bethany, you can sit at Jesus' feet and listen to God's Word. It is a mindful, Christ-focused quieting. I realize that for some, using terms like, "Lord, have mercy," or "Christ, have mercy," in this setting might be disruptive to them, so you can make this an individual choice. Merely breathing consciously will suffice.

By *pausing internal self-conversation*, you have the opportunity to *let go* of ingrained emotional-response habits and behaviors and hear the power of God's Word within you. A healing and restructured emotional-response pattern can begin, but it's now directed by the Holy Spirit. We come to God's Word quietly and unhurriedly to hear God's *whisper*, to open ourselves to the working of the Holy Spirit within our hearts, and to understand God's good will for us as beloved children.

The prayer:

1. Listening to the Word: As you are quieted, then offer a prayer inviting the Holy Spirit into your time of being in God's Word, asking that the Holy Spirit work God's Word and will within you. Theologians like Luther suggest reading the Word aloud so that it is heard not just by your heart, but also upon your ears.

2. Discursive meditation: Having quieted and received the Word of God, now you are praying in God's own words, in God's language, and doing so in the presence of the Holy Spirit. In this second phase of Word-saturated meditative prayer, we discursively meditate on God's Word. We can reflect on the entire text of the chosen passage, or even just a word or two of the Scripture for the day. One might allow several minutes for this time of reflection in the presence of the Spirit.

3. Praying God's will: Through the Spirit, God has worked the Word within us. However, we know that the forces of sin are also always present, tempting to separate us from the love of God. Therefore we begin a time of praying God's Word and will into our specific intentions, concerns, struggles, and yes, our praise, thanks and

celebrations of life. Here we ask that God's will, as expressed in our meditation on the Word, be applied to our daily faith-walk. We know that Satan, the desires of the world, and our own flesh will tempt us to try to separate us from our relationship with God.

4. Rest: We then take just a moment in Part Four to rest securely in the Word, being held in the arms of our Savior, the Good Shepherd. Being refreshed by being in God's holy Word, we may be guided back into the Scriptures for further reflection, or be released into the activities of our day.

On our Grace Place Wellness Retreats (www.graceplacewellness.org) we suggest three cycles of this meditative prayer format. First, we read the Scripture text aloud and meditate on the entire chosen text for the day. In the second cycle, again reading the text aloud, we focus on just a word or phrase from the text on which to reflect silently under the guidance of the Holy Spirit. Third, because we do this in a group setting, after reading the text aloud, we take time to share our meditation aloud with each other, to receive insight from those journeying with us. Often we close the third cycle with the Lord's Prayer focused on God's will being done in our lives and for our time of personal intention.

The direction and focus is to breathe in and within the Scriptures throughout the entire prayer, including adding a moment of rest as we prepare to return to a reading of God's Word. Our intention and direction is to invite God to work the Word within us, whether actively, as the Holy Spirit guides us during the time of quiet meditation on the Word, or passively as in the time of rest, simply opening ourselves up to God to fill us with God's presence as expressed in the Word and quietly pause to dwell in God's love for us. God is giving; we are receiving. We eat, drink, and inwardly digest God's messages of comfort, love, peace, and joy.

You can add a moment of reflective song to close your time of Word-saturated meditative prayer. For many, that can be the singing of a verse or two of a familiar hymn, or a Christian-based song. Here again, let me offer some familiar hymns and songs:

My Faith Looks Up to Thee

O God, Our Help in Ages Past

Jesus, Grant That Balm and Healing

Your Hand, O Lord, in Days of Old

Be Still, My Soul

You Who Dwell in the Shelter of the Lord

I Leave All Things to God's Direction

When in the Hour of Deepest Need

A Mighty Fortress Is Our God

Turn Your Eyes upon Jesus

Breathe on Me, Breath of God

Finally, go in peace and serve the Lord throughout your day.

There are many wonderful resources for reading and learning more about meditative prayer.

1. Search for "Oratio, Meditatio, Tentatio" and "Martin Luther"—for example, "Oratio, Meditatio, Tentatio: What Makes a Theologian," *Concordia Theological Quarterly* 66/3 (2002): 255-67 or www.johnkleinig.com.

2. Search for topics under "contemplative outreach" and "Father Thomas Keating"—for example, at www.contemplativeoutreach.org.

3. Examine multiple texts or articles exploring Lectio Divina by St. Augustine, such as "Ever Ancient, Ever New: The Art and Practice of Lectio Divina" at www.usccb.org.

ENDNOTES

1. Cognition: This is the mental process of acquiring knowledge and understanding through our thought, experience, and our senses. Cognition includes our memory, attention, knowledge, judgment, reasoning, problem-solving, language, and decision-making activities.

2. *Unraveling the Mysteries of Anxiety and its Disorders from the Perspective of Emotion Theory*, David H. Barlow, American Psychologist, p. 55, 2000.

3. Ego: A model of the apparatus of the human psyche developed by Sigmund Freud. He theorized three interactive components; the **id** is a group of uncoordinated instinctual trends in the psyche; the **super-ego** plays a most critical, moralizing role; and the **ego** is the realistic, organized component of psyche that mediates between the desires of the id and the **super-ego.**

4. *Teach Yourself Freud*, Ruth Snowden, McGraw-Hill, 2008, pp 105-107.

5. Grace Place Wellness Ministries (GPW) is a faith-based wellness organization housed in St. Louis, Missouri. The mission and vision for GPW is to "nurture vitality and joy in ministry by inspiring and equipping church workers to lead healthy lives." This is accomplished by GPW through providing wellness-focused retreats, lectures, religious organizational and congregational seminars, and wellness consultations, all across this country and abroad to professional church leaders, workers, faith families, and missionaries. To learn more about GPW, please visit www.graceplacewellness.org.

6. *Confessions: A New Translation*, Henry Chadwick, Oxford World Classics, 2009.

7. *"Let all bitterness and wrath and anger and clamor and slander be put away from you, along with all malice."* (Ephesians 4:31, ESV) Look at a few other translations of this cascade. The New Living Translation (NLT) states, *"...bitterness, rage, anger, harsh words, and slander, as well as all types of evil behavior."* The King James Version reads, *"... bitterness, and wrath, and anger, and clamor, and evil speaking, be put away from you with all malice."*

8. Text © 1982 Concordia Publishing House. Used with permission. www.cph.org.

9. *The Lord's Supper: Five Verses*, Gordon T. Smith, IVP Academic, 2008.

10. Contact me at www.graceplacewellness.org or 314-842-3077.

11. For more on the congregational or denominational health from a systems theory of organizations, explore the writings of Ron W. Richardson: Creating a Healthier Church: Family Systems Theory, Leadership, and Congregational Life, Fortress Press, 1995; or Peter L. Steinke: Healthy Congregations: A Systems Approach, Rowman & Littlefield, 2006.

12. We can garner some wonderful insights into this counseling process from a secular text in a worthwhile read entitled The Anatomy of Peace: Resolving the Heart of Conflict, second edition, The Arbinger Institute, Berrett-Koehler Publishers, 2015.

13. Ambassadors of Reconciliation is an international ministry founded to help Christians and their churches in carrying out their peacemaking responsibilities. They equip Christian leaders for living, proclaiming, and cultivating lifestyles of reconciliation. The ministry of reconciliation is given to the local church and every believer. Ambassadors of Reconciliation purposes to inspire and prepare the leaders of Christ's Church around the world in carrying out this vocation in more effective ways. Ambassadors of

Reconciliation serves proactively through teaching and offering resources such as books, Bible studies, devotions, and more. They train church leaders through seminars and practicums. The ministry assists people in conflict through reconciliation services and licensed counseling. Their experienced reconcilers coach individuals in conflict, mediate disputing parties, and arbitrate substantive issues. In addition they offer group reconciliation services, leadership consultation, and professional counseling. You can learn more from their website at www.hisaor.org.

14. For further reading see *Dialogues in Clinical Neuroscience:* "A History of Anxiety: From Hippocrates to DSM," 2015.

OTHER BOOKS BY JOHN D. ECKRICH, M.D.

Vocation and Wellness:
Renew Your Energy for Christian Living

Available in print and e-book formats at online retailers.

Visit www.graceplacewellness.org for more information.